THE MONSOON CLOUD

POET KĀḶAMĒKAM AND
HIS IRREVERENT POETRY

The New Ecology of Expressive Modes in Early-Modern South India (or NEEM) series explores the major expressive domains—literature, music, painting, sculpture, architecture, dance, philosophical thought—in the languages and cultures of south India, including Sanskrit and Persian, from the sixteenth to the early nineteenth century. The unifying idea weaving together these volumes is that all of south India constituted a single, integrated, multi-lingual cultural system during this period, and was connected by common themes and socio-economic-political processes. It is evident that a civilizational shift was taking place at this time, and that new notions of scientific knowledge, the nature of self and mind, concepts of space, time, and history, and the meaning of being human—among other themes—were crystallizing in the languages and cultural settings of south India.

The NEEM series has emerged from the European Research Council's five-year project at the Hebrew University, under the European Union's Horizon 2020 Research and Innovation Programme. A series of monographs have been envisaged in collaboration with Primus Books as part of this project.

NEW ECOLOGY OF EXPRESSIVE MODES IN EARLY-MODERN SOUTH INDIA

Series Editor David Shulman

Other titles in this series:

Introspection and Insight: South Indian Minds in the Early Common Era
DAVID SHULMAN

Kutiyattam: The Long History that Memory Keeps [Continuities and Transformations of a Theatre Tradition into the Twenty-first Century]
SUDHA GOPALAKRISHNAN

The Knife, the Parrot, the Beam, and the Jar: Continuity and Change in the Ritual of Tēvāram in Kerala
ELENA MUCCIARELLI

Printers, Preachers and Princes: Cultures of Literary Patronage in Early Modern and Colonial South India
CEZARY GALEWICZ

The Pāṭṭu Century in Carnatic Music
NARESH KEERTHI

When Sanskrit Sought Range: The Literary, the Colloquial, and the Classical in Early Modern Maratha Thanjavur
TALIA ARIAV

The Lilatilakam *Grammar of Manipravalam*
SIVAN GOREN-ARZONY

The Many Truths of Vācaspati Miśra and Appayya Dīkṣita: Scholarly Versatility, Philosophical Pluralism, and Religious Alliances
DMITRY SHEVCHENKO

NEW ECOLOGY OF EXPRESSIVE MODES
IN EARLY-MODERN SOUTH INDIA

The Monsoon Cloud

POET KĀḶAMĒKAM AND HIS IRREVERENT POETRY

Suganya Anandakichenin

PRIMUS BOOKS
An imprint of Ratna Sagar P. Ltd.
Virat Bhavan, Mukherjee Nagar Commercial Complex
Delhi 110 009

Offices at CHENNAI LUCKNOW
AGRA AHMEDABAD BENGALURU BHOPAL COIMBATORE
DEHRADUN GUWAHATI HYDERABAD JAIPUR JALANDHAR
KANPUR KOCHI KOLKATA MUMBAI PATNA RANCHI VARANASI

First published 2024

ISBN: 978-93-5852-833-6 (Paperback)
ISBN: 978-93-5852-768-1 (PoD)

Published by Primus Books

Laser typeset by Mithu Karmakar
Digicon Edutech Services

This project has received funding from the European Research Council (ERC) under the European Union's Horizon 2020 Research and Innovation Programme (grant agreement no. 786083 - NEEM).

Contents

Foreword

Kāḷamekappulavar, still a household name in the Tamil country, occupies a niche of his own in the history of Tamil literature. He belongs to the fifteenth century; he is perhaps the only Tamil poet to be mentioned by name, or by epithet, in a contemporaneous temple inscription. We can thus be quite sure that there was such a person. Suganya Anandakichinen's book is the first full, pioneering study of this poet and his oeuvre, in any language.

It is not by chance that he appeared during a time of radical systemic change in the south, generally, and in the Tamil country in particular. Such moments inevitably generate eccentric artists who delineate, and at the same time subvert and transcend, the boundaries and conventions of an earlier age. Kāḷamēkam follows upon the major narrative poems such as Kampaṉ's *Irāmāvatāram* and Pukaḻentippulavar's *Naḷavĕṇpā*, both associated with the Chola (in Pukaḻenti's case, the late-Chola) courtly production. By the fifteenth century, with the Tamil country now under the partial control of Telugu-speaking Vijayanagara warriors, we find early examples of the lyrical and linguistically complex 'Short Genres' (*cirr'ilakkiyam*) as well as a wealth of stand-alone verses, *taṉippāṭal* or *cāṭu/muktaka*.

Kāḷamēkam composed in both of these modes, though it is the short stand-alone verses that are best known today. They are, without exception, linguistic *tours de force*—almost unthinkable, miraculous constructions, playful, sometimes enigmatic or riddling, and always seen by the Tamil tradition as extempore creations. Kāḷamēkam embodies the poetic ideal, largely new to this period, of the *ācu kavi*, the 'quick-witted' poet, directly linked to the goddess Sarasvatī and thus capable of improvising a complex poem more or less without thinking. Such a poet is also thought to be omniscient. It is possible that this description of the profession was, in fact, true to life, as examples we know from the nineteenth century would suggest.

But it is not just a matter of quick wit and a total mastery of the Tamil language (and its canonical corpus). A poet like Kāḷamēkam is also a kind of sorcerer, magically potent, who can combine syllables and metremes in a modular verbal utterance that can kill an enemy, cause the subject of the poem to fall helplessly in love, heal the sick, even revive the dead. Such word-magic was definitely a useful tool for the little kings and zamindars who cropped up in this period as patrons. In some sense, the political domain depended to no small degree on the *ācu kavi*'s presence and mastery of language. In terms of literary history, we find in Kāḷamēkam's verses, and especially in the revealing stories that are told about them and whatever triggered them, a tonality that runs the whole range from mild or pointed irony (*muraṇpāṭu*) to mocking sarcasm (*kiṇṭal, naiyāṇṭi*, among other terms) to bitter, biting rebuke (*vacai*) and potentially deadly curses. Systemic breakdown and innovation regularly drift toward reflexive irony as earlier modes of speaking, singing, and thinking begin to lose their grip. It is not always easy to understand that tonality (especially on first hearing), given its prevalent features of paranomasia, deliberate obscurity, unusual lexis, staggered syntax, and the characteristic south Indian counterpoint of metrical-musical and verbal poetry. Stated more simply: one dependable component of beauty in pre-modern Tamil poems is the way sentences, or indeed all kinds of verbal strings, are at odds with the meter in which they are sung. Once such pregnant poems are deciphered by the listener, she experiences both aesthetic joy and psychic relief.

The reader is about to encounter many such poems in Suganya's translations (together with the Tamil original, for those who can read it). With the poems come the often dramatic, even terrifying stories that the tradition has woven around them. Verses like these open up an entire cultural world, clearly evolving toward the revolution in literary and musical taste in early modern times. Figures like Kāḷamēkam foreshadow, and in some ways prepared the ground, for that revolution. This book is thus a study in the cultural and intellectual history of the far south in a period of rapid transition and continuous experimentation in political and social life, in language, in notions of personhood and gender roles, and in metaphysical meditation, all of the above clearly evident in a still emergent sensibility.

DAVID SHULMAN

CHAPTER ONE

Introducing Kāḷamēkam

Who was Kāḷamēkam?

vacai pāṭa kāḷamēkam–'Kāḷamēkam for singing satires'
—ANONYMOUS

If I sit, I sit. If I rise,
I'm a great monsoon cloud/Kāḷamēkam, o child! (9)[1]

THUS THUNDERS A Tamil poet known for the swiftness of his poetry-making and his imaginative, clever poetry. This notoriously irascible poet Kāḷamēkam is known for his impromptu poetry-making and his satirical verse, so much so that Kamil Zvelebil (1974: 53) calls him 'the only Tamil writer of the past who can claim the name of satirist!' Eminent Tamil scholar Aruṇācalam (2005 [1969]: 31) points out how popular the poet still was among learned and non-learned people alike.[2] Although popularly known

---

[1]The whole verse is translated later on. See Chapter 2, section 'Pride and Sensitivity'.

[2]He also adds that interest in such works was waning in general. Interestingly, Aruṇācalam (1944: 27) states in his introduction to the poet's other extant work, the *Tiruvānaikkā Ulā*, that the uneducated Tamil people from the countryside without

for his legendary *vacai* ('satirical') verses, his poetry also shows his poetic genius and absolute mastery over the Tamil language, while betraying his fiery spirit and fine understanding of the human psyche. This book hopes to help the reader discover Kāḷamēkam's brilliant poetry, and in the process, to know more about the poet, what he was, what he saw and thought about what he saw, how he felt about certain things, what he said and what he left unsaid, and how all this allows us to better understand the man behind the poet.

Stories about Kāḷamēkam abound, but there is very little reliable information, which is hardly surprising given the fact that even the most famous Tamil poets and their lives are relatively unknown to us.[3] Since other reliable evidence such as inscriptions that mention the poets is scarce in this part of the world, we have to rely on intertextual references, as well as linguistic, historical, and other such clues that are found scattered across the original text. Perhaps this lack of authentic knowledge about the lives of the poets is the reason why even non-religious poets are often treated like their religious counterparts and the saints (whether the latter were composers or not): their biographies, often based on the remnants of collective memory, the imaginative interpretations of

---

an 'English education' and not too much of a 'Tamil education' either, would still quote Kāḷamēkam's *taṉippāṭal*s.

[3]We can give the example of Kampaṉ, who, despite being one of the most renowned Tamil poets, is hard to date with certainty and whose life is hard to know about with any accuracy. U. Vē. Cāmiṉātaiyar (1950) (among others) expresses his frustration at the false attributions while discussing this issue.

their words, and the biographers' fantasy, are at best hagiographic in nature, for as Srilata Raman (2022: 5) rightly points out, hagiography was the first choice in the premodern period when it came to narrating the lives of 'kings or saints, cultural heroes, or low-caste figures'. We can add eminent poets to this list, which makes it a challenge to separate fact from fiction; often, fiction leaves no space for any fact at all. But I digress. Who was Kāḷamēkam? And when did he live? What was he like?

A few works mention Kāḷamēkam and/or quote verses attributed to him (e.g. Paṭikkācu Pulavar's seventeenth-century *Toṇṭai maṇṭala catakam*, verses 79 and 80, respectively). But they do not tell us much about the poet himself. Most of what we know about him (or think that we do!), apart from what he says himself, comes from late accounts of his life. For, although he seems to have lived in the fifteenth century, his story was apparently not told till the modern period—at least not in writing. And most such works were a compilation of life stories of a set of poets, often beginning with Caṅkam bards going all the way up to the eighteenth/nineteenth-century poets. One such early narration of Kāḷamēkam's life story is made by the *Viṉōtaracasamañcari* (henceforth, *Mañcari*)[4] composed by Aṭṭāvatāṉam Vīrācāmic Ceṭṭiyār. Rather than tell his story in a straightforward way, this work actually gives the context to about ninety of his verses, mostly (but not only) of those composed to satisfy specific requests (*camicai/saṃjñās*), as the title to the chapter

---

[4]Aruṇācalam (2005 [1969]: 33) states that this work—a collection of stories transmitted through oral sources till it was first published in 1876—is the first to narrate Kāḷamēkam's story.

itself suggests: 'The *camicai*s set individually by Atimaturakavi and the sixty-four *taṇṭikai* poets,[5] and the songs that Poet Kāḷamēkam composed'.[6] It also offers an explanation of those verses in simple Tamil prose, although it leaves out the ones that are too 'saucy' (*iṭakkarkaḷ*) and harshly insulting (*koṭiya vacai*). It is almost as if the author is providing a *kiḷavi* ('theme, subject') for some of Kāḷamēkam's verses, just like the ones prefixed to the Caṅkam verses, probably long after they were composed. For, without a context, it is not always easy to make sense of some of his verses. Other biographies of poets include the seventeenth-century (?) *Tamiḻ Nāvalar Caritai*[7] and the nineteenth-century *Pulavar Purāṇam* by Taṇṭapāṇi Cuvāmikaḷ.[8]

Before we examine these works and the poet's own words, it is appropriate to begin with an inscription found in the Kāmākṣī temple that apparently mentions him, or at least a certain *kāḷamukil* ('black/monsoon cloud'), which scholars such as the

---

[5]It would seem that a poet who receives a *taṇṭikai* 'palanquin' from a king or a chieftain as a reward for their poetry was known as a *taṇṭikai* poet.

[6]'*atimaturakaviyum aṟupattunālu taṇṭikaippulavarkaḷum taṉittaṉi koṭutta camicaikaḷum kāḷamēkappulavar pāṭiya pāṭalkaḷum*'.

[7]An earlier work, the *Tamiḻ Nāvalar Caritai*, was 'cleaned up' and published again in the nineteenth/early twentieth century. Nāyakar (1921: ii–iii), its editor, tentatively suggests that it might have been composed around two-and-a-half centuries earlier (i.e. approximately 1671). Narrating the life-stories of Tamil poets, the *Caritai* simply lists verses by Kāḷamēkam, twenty-two to be precise, preceded by a title that gives each verse's gist. However, it is not clear whether the titles are editorial additions or if the original author had included them.

[8]Chapter 56 of this work contains sixty-eight verses in Tamil on Kāḷamēkam.

eminent archaeologist Nākacuvāmi (also spelt as R. Nagaswamy) (1976: 39) and Mu. Aruṇācalam (2005 [1969]: 36) believe to be a reference to our poet.[9] The former describes his emotions at discovering this inscription and his growing conviction that the inscribed verses were by Kāḷamēkam himself, who is also mentioned in them:

I read there the name *kāḷamukil* in the end. Unconsciously, I had a feeling—a [sense of] delight—[of] joy. I told my students that *kāḷamukil* refers to Kāḷamēkam. I could not stand there anymore. I quickly ran towards my seat and sat down. It took a few seconds for that agitation to subside. The joy that I was now seeing for the very first time, in an inscription, a poet that I had only heard about so far by means of literature—[I felt] an unspeakable joy! I went back and read the other inscribed verses too. I felt every second that my conviction was gaining in strength. (Nagaswamy 1976: 39–40)[10]

[9] The verse inscribed on the Kanchipuram temple wall, dated to the seventeenth century by Kō. Ceṅkūṭṭuvaṉ (2017: n.p.) is, the following:

maṉṉil iruvar maṇavāḷar maṉṉ aḷanta/ kaṇṇaṉavaṉ ivaṉ pēr kāḷamukil-
*   kaṇṇaṉ/*
avaṉukk' ūr eṇṇil aṇiy araṅkam oṉṟē/ ivaṉukk' ūr eṇṇāyiram.

'There are two bridegrooms on [this] earth: that Kṛṣṇa who measured the world, and the name of this one (i.e. me) is monsoon cloud [-like?] Kṛṣṇa. If one thinks of that [Kṛṣṇa's] town, it is the ornate Śrīraṅgam. This one's town is Eṇṇāyiram/ eight thousand cities'.

[10] *irutiyil atil 'kāḷ amukil' eṉṟa peyaruip paṭittēṉ. ennai aṟiyātu oru uṇarcci – uvakai - makiḻcci. kāḷ amukil eṉpatu kāḷ amēkattaik kuṟikkum ena eṉ māṇavarkaḷiṭam kūṟiṉēṉ. ataṟkumēl eṉṉāl aṅku niṟka muṭiyavillai, viṭuviṭu eṉru ōṭi vantu eṉ irukkaiyil amarntuviṭṭēṉ. cila viṉāṭikaḷ āyiṟru, anta paṭapaṭappu aṭaṅkuvataṟku. itukāṟum ilakkiya vāyilākavē kēṭṭirunta oru pulavaṉai, ippolutu kalveṭṭil mutaṉmutalāka nām pārkkiṟōm eṉra makiḻvu - collat teriyāta makiḻvu. mīṇṭum tirumpic ceṉru, piṟa pāṭal*

Because we do not know any other poet called *kāḷamukil* and because another verse (probably a floating one) refers to him by means of this very epithet,[11] chances are that Nagaswamy is right, although this inscription does not really help us narrow down our poet's date, except to provide the seventeenth century as the *terminus ad quem*.

Apart from this, we also have a verse, likely by a contemporary of Kāḷamēkam, which a few scholars attribute to the *iraṭṭai pulavar* ('twin poets', *c.* fifteenth century), and which seems to be a *kaiyaṟunilai* poem that describes 'the utter helplessness of dependents at the death of a chief' (*Madras Tamil Lexicon*, henceforth, MTL); s.v. *kaiyaṟunilai*), a kind of *caramakavi* ('elegy'):

---

kalveṭṭukkaḷ aiyum paṭittēṉ. eṉ karuttu valippaṭṭu varuvatākavē ovvoru viṉāṭiyum uṇarntēṉ.

In a personal communication (dated February 2023), Professor K. Nachimuthu told me that this inscription has not been published yet.

[11]The following floating verse, quoted by Nagaswamy (1976: 40), shows that the name *kāḷamukil*, a synonym of Kāḷamēkam, has been used in poetry to refer to the poet:

kācukkuk kampaṉ karuṇaikk' aruṇakiri/ ācukkuk kāḷamukil-āvaṉē − tēcu perum
ūlukkuk kūttaṉ uvakkap pukalēnti/ kūḷukk' iṅk' auvaiyeṉak kūṟu.

'Say that Kampaṉ is [the best] for *kācu*; Aruṇakiri[nātar], for compassion; Kāḷamukil, for extempore verses; the brilliant Kūttaṉ, for *karma*[-like words that come true]; Pukalēnti, for [our] delight, [and] Auvai, for gruel here'.

Please note that in prosody, *kācu* means 'a formula of a foot of two nēr acai (--), the latter ending in 'u', occurring in the last foot of a veṇpā' (*Madras Tamil Lexicon*), and also that there is a story around Auvai composing some verse because she had accepted gruel from someone.

O Monsoon cloud/Kāḷamēkam whose renown spreads all over
   the world
thanks to extempore verses! O god upon the earth (brahmin)!
Your mouth that said *maṇ tinṟa pāṇam*
Is burning in the red fire that took the sky, alas! Alas![12]

This verse is clearly dedicated to our poet, whom it
names explicitly and calls an *ācukavi*, one who could
compose extempore verses, which he apparently did
abundantly. It also indicates that he was a brahmin,
and attributes a verse to him, which contains the words
maṇ tinṟa pāṇam. A variant of this elegiac verse, with
the first two lines containing a couple of pertinent
differences, is attributed to another poet whom we
briefly met earlier on, Atimaturakavi (Puliyūr 2010:
ii[13]), although neither its authorship nor its date of
composition can be authenticated easily:

O Varada from Nandi with fragrant paddy-fields!
   O poet Kāḷamēkam/Monsoon cloud
That spreads in all quarters! O god upon the earth (brahmin)!

[12]*ācu kaviyāl akilav ulak' eṅkum/ vīcu pukaḻk kāḷamēkamē! – pūcurā!/
viṇ koṇṭa centaṉal-āy vēkutēy, aiyaiyō!/ 'maṇ ṭinṟa pāṇam' enṟa vāy.*
Please note that the author of the *Mañcari* (p. 266) does not
accept the authorship of the *iraṭṭai pulavar* but suggests some
other (anonymous) learned person; and the verse that he gives
contains a variant in the first two lines, although the meaning is
more or less unchanged:

   ācu kavi māri akila ulakam ellām/ vīcu kavi kāḷamēkamē pūcurā

'O Poet Kāḷamēkam who spreads showers of extempore verses
   all over the world! O god upon the earth (brahmin)!'

For a brief discussion on this verse, see Rao and Shulman 1998:
14–16.
   [13]Although Puliyūr names Mu. Irākavaiyaṅkār as his source,
since he does not give precise bibliographic information, I have
not been able to trace it.

Why is [your] mouth that said *maṇ tiṉṟa pāṇam*
Burning in the harsh fire that eats up the useless, o wretch![14]

This version adds a different set of information, namely, that the poet's name was Varataṉ, and that he came from a town called Nanti (probably Nantipuram near Kumbhakonam). While the poet seems to call himself by that name on one occasion (v. 212; see fn19, it is not clear how this town came to be associated with him. To add to this, based on personal communication, U. Vē. Cāminātaiyar, perhaps the most eminent Tamil scholar of the 20th century, known as *tamiḻ tāttā* ('grandfather of Tamil'), suggests (in Vaittiyanātaṉ 1986: 111) that the poet lived in Cittāmpūr, where he took up residence after receiving rewards from Tirumalai Rāyaṉ.[15]

If we turn our attention to the 'biographic' works, they too state that Kāḷamēkam was a brahmin, possibly a

---

[14]*vācavayal nanti varatā ticaiyaṉaittum/ vīcu kavikāḷa mēkamē —
pūcurā/ vīṇtiṉṟa vevvaḻavil vēkutē pāviyēṉ maṇtiṉṟa pāṇameṉṟa vāy.*

[15]His source, Śrīrāmaiyar from Citta(?ā)mpūr, also asserts that Kāḷamēkam built and donated twenty-four houses for twenty-four brahmins, and that he (Śrīrāmaiyar) was a descendant of one of those families that had moved in. He adds that Kāḷamēkam built himself a house too and settled down in that town. To back this up, he quotes a verse that his elders claimed was Kāḷamēkam's, in which he sings in praise of the local Gaṇeśa. That verse, which mentions Cittāmpūr, does not seem to be extant anymore. According to Śrīrāmaiyar, the brahmins' quarter, the *agrahāra*, was named 'Kāḷamēkam teru'. Śrīrāmaiyar also claims that Kāḷamēkam composed a poem in the dramatic *kuṟavañci* (or some such) genre dedicated to Tyāgarāja of Tiruvārūr, and that proof of that got damaged with time. Fragments of such memories are precious, for often, those are the only things that we are left with, if at all.

Śrīvaiṣṇava one[16] who served at the Śrīraṅgam temple and switched to Śaivism to please his concubine, a devadasi[17] from the nearby Tiruvāṉaikkā temple (*Mañcari*, p. 219). This, the biographers insinuate, explains the convert's zeal evident in his poems that belittle Viṣṇu vis-à-vis Śiva. Also like any poet worth the name, traditions suggest that he obtained his poetic prowess from the Devī of Tiruvāṉaikkā (Sarasvatī according to other sources, including Zvelebil's [1974: 53]), who spit betel leaf juice into his mouth, thus turning a simple man into a great poet, which also gives him 'the power to make reality conform to his or her speech' (Rao and Shulman 1998: 11). And, in order to thank her, he composed the *Tiruvāṉaikkā Ulā*. This story is reminiscent of parallel stories narrated about other poets like Kālidāsa, but also about a later Tamil poet called Āṇṭāṉ Kavirāyaṉ, whom we shall meet again later. Kāḷamēkam is also said to have challenged poet Atimaturam,[18] apparently an arrogant (or is it jealous?) court poet of Tirumalai Rāyaṉ's, to a rough and tough contest known as *yamakaṇṭam-pāṭutal* in which the poets had to compose verses that fit the *camicai*s given to them, and which could end in the loss of life of either contestant (usually the losing one).

---

[16]Or a Vaṭamaṉ Smārta brahmin according to the *Mañcari*, p. 219, although its author does not provide any further explanations as to how he came to that conclusion.

[17]To know more about the devadasis in Tamilnadu and about how the perception of devadasis and their roles changed in society over many centuries, see Orr 2000.

[18]Not many verses attributed to Atimaturakavi (except perhaps a couple, namely, the one quoted above and another in Chapter 2, section 'Pride and sensitivity') have been found now.

So what do we even know for sure about this Kāḷamēkam? Although I will try to become acquainted with the man behind the poetic façade throughout this book, I will attempt to glean whatever biographic information I can from his own words, how the modern scholars have interpreted them, and present that in this chapter. At this point, it is essential to keep in mind that quite a few of the verses attributed to our poet may not be his, which takes us to the issues of interpolations, lack of a critical edition, and so forth, which we shall deal with later.

To begin with, Kāḷamēkam gives what seems to be his birth name (Varatan̲, v. 212[19]) in a love epistle, but he more frequently uses his epithet/title/nom de plume, Kāḷamēkam ('monsoon cloud', v. 9). It is worth noting that both are Vaiṣṇava names: Varatan̲ is the short form of Varadarājan̲, the name of the main deity in the Varadarāja-Viṣṇu temple in Kāñcīpuram (of whom he sings in v. 107), and Kāḷamēkam is the main deity in Tirumōkūr near Madurai, to whom he dedicates a verse as well (v. 82). This information has given rise to a few pertinent hypotheses, which we shall briefly explore now. N. Śrītaran̲ (2013: 6), one of the modern editors of Kāḷamēkam's poetry, asserts that the poet belonged to the *pūrvaśikhā* Cōḻiya

---

[19]*nal̠l̠ār̠r̠ut toṇṭikku nal varatan̲ tūṭṭu maṭal/ vil̠l̠āmal ettan̲ai nāl̠empuvēn̲-kal̠l̠a*
 matan̲ap payal oruvan̲ vantu poruñ caṇṭaikku/ utavak kaṭuki varavum.
  212

'[This] is a letter that good Varatan̲ is composing for Toṇṭi from Nal̠l̠ār̠u. For how long will I be distressed in mind without speaking out? Come swiftly to help [me] in the battle that the cunning Kāma fellow is waging!'

brahmin community (which wears the tuft to the fore), the only one that gives the name 'Kāḷamēkam' to its children. He adds that Kāḷamēkam's scolding of a Cōḻiya brahmin in such an uninhibited way in v. 189 (see Chapter 2, section titled 'Anger, Humour, Wit') proves this point.[20] This is as good a hypothesis as any other, such as believing this epithet to be a title that he acquired for his poetic skills (e.g. *Mañcari*, p. 220). Śrītaraṉ (2013: 5) also suggests that the poet's father may have been a cook in the Tirumōkūr temple kitchen (*maṭaippaḷḷi*), and that due to poverty, the poet himself may have given him a hand, which would explain his almost obsessive interest in food (see Chapter 2, section titled 'Anger, Humour, Wit').[21] It has also been suggested that he may have joined the kitchen of the Śrīraṅgam temple, the most important place of worship for the Śrīvaiṣṇavas with a large Śrīvaiṣṇava community inhabiting it since at least the beginning of the second millennium. This explains his knowledge of and remarks about the tension between the Śaivas and Vaiṣṇavas in the region, for he clearly mentions the bickering between the temple workers

[20]It is strange that having used this verse (*cutukku/corukku*) as an argument to illustrate his point, Śrītaraṉ does not even seem to include it in his edition.

[21]In v. 196, he addresses a mango and wonders why it did not become pickled by Āccāḷ; in v. 194, he praises the meal served by a certain Amarapatiyār by detailing the menu (and including puns in the process); in v.193, he lavishes with praise a priest from Tiruppaṉantāḷ for his generosity in serving food; three of his verses (v. 46, 192, 195), some of which are dealt with in this book, mocks women who could not cook properly. There are other verses in which he expresses discontent when he could not get food or eat it peacefully.

at Śrīraṅgam and Tiruvānaikkā, which hosts an important shrine for Śiva, with the two temple towns being located barely a couple of kilometres away from each other.[22] While Kālamēkam may indeed have been born a Śrīvaiṣṇava, it is very clear that he did not remain one, as his preference for Śiva over Viṣṇu is obvious from his tendency to praise the former and belittle the latter in his poetry (see Chapter 3, section titled 'Establishing the Supremacy of the Favourite God: *Nindā* and *Stuti*'). He also reserves a harsher tone for the latter and for the people and places related to him.

Also, if indeed Kālamēkam was a Cōḻiya brahmin and the son of a temple cook (and himself following in that path if only for a while), this could explain something of his aggressive tone, for the Cōḻiya brahmins were (still are?) considered inferior by other more orthodox brahmins, as Walter G. Neevel (1977: 84) points out.[23] For someone naturally talented and proud (as a result of that talent, probably), lack of recognition—or even respect—among his peers (perhaps aggravated by his occupation and financial status) may have furthered a sense of alienation. And this may have both given an edge to this tongue and

[22]The poet definitely mentions a conflict between the neighbouring temple towns, and read in a certain way, he also indicates his devotion for Śiva. See v. 143 in Chapter 4.

[23]'The Coḻiya Brahmans [are] a relatively ancient class in South India (associated in some way with the Cola kings or region) whose status was low among the orthodox because of its close associations with such popular Non-Vedic movements as Tantric temple worship and the largely non-Brahmanic Tamil hymnic Bhakti movement.'

even driven him into the arms of the common man, irrespective of their caste, for he does write about people from different backgrounds and social classes, although he does not seem to question the concept of caste itself. A man of his times, Kāḷamēkam simply accepted the order of things as he found them in the society that he lived in: he feels keenly injustice meted out at him, but is not necessarily angered by what is done to the others. For example, in a special kind of verse called *kaṭaimoḻi mārru* (literally, switching the last word; see Puliyūr 2010: 55), which requires the last word of the verse to be placed at its beginning for the verse to make sense, Kāḷamēkam lists a few caste names and what jobs the people belonging to them do:

> *māṭu tiṉpāṉ pārppāṉ maṟaiyōtuvāṉ kuyavaṉ*
> *kūṭi mika maṉ picaivāṉ kollaṉē—tēṭi*
> *irump' aṭippāṉ cekkāṉ eṇṇey viṟpāṉ vaṇṇāṉ*
> *parum puṭavai tappum paṟai 83.*[24]

This is a tentative translation that gives an idea of how this verse reads to a Tamil audience:

> eats beef—the brahmin,
> recites the Vedas—the potter,
> gathers soil and kneads [it]—the smith,
> seeks iron and beats [it]—the worker of oil-press,
> sells oil—the washerman,
> beats the heavy saree—the Pariah.

If we move the last word to the initial position, the verse reads thus, as the poet intended it:

[24]Please note that I will quote the verse in its original language in the main body of the text if I find it essential to grasp the pun, the alliteration, and so forth. On other occasions, I will merely give the verses in Tamil in the notes.

> The Pariah eats beef—
> the brahmin recites the Vedas—
> the potter gathers soil and kneads [it]—
> the smith seeks iron and beats [it]—
> the worker of oil-press sells oil—
> the washerman beats the heavy saree.

Kāḷamēkam is not critical of the social order, but just describes it as it was in his times or perhaps even repeats clichés (e.g. the lower caste people's food habits). He also speaks of women based on how they were perceived in the society of their times, and does not at any point question those assumptions (see Chapter 2, section titled 'Kāḷamēkam's Values and Worldview'). He does not question some people being wealthier than others either, although he does lament his own poverty (v. 6; see fn 27). On one rare occasion, however, he bitingly criticizes the rise of prices that makes the lives of women hard (v. 203).[25] So, our largely apolitical Kāḷamēkam is not a revolutionary

---

[25]This is one of the few occasions (perhaps even the only occasion) when the poet is stirred into standing up for the downtrodden:

taṇṭāṅkūr mā canaṅkāḷ! carkuṇar nīr eṉr' iruntēṉ!/ paṇṭam kuṟaiya viṟṟa pāvikāḷ! peṇṭukaḷait
tēṭiy uṇṇa viṭṭīr terukkaḷ terukkaḷ-toṟum/ āṭi mutal āṉivaraikkum. 203

O great people of Taṇṭāṅkūr! I had thought that you were of
    a good nature! O sinners who sell lesser [quantity] of
    provisions [at the same price]!
You have made the women forage for food in each and every
    street from [the month of] Āṭi to Āṉi!

Please note that the month of Āṉi is followed by Āṭi, which means that according to the poet, the problem persists throughout the year. One may also wonder what the women were pushed to do in order to survive, especially since he mentions the streets.

poet, although that is a trend often found in some of his influential poetic counterparts, such as the Cittars.[26] As a matter of fact, he even uses a caste-based insult (*pulaiyā* 'outcaste', v. 189) to insult a fellow brahmin (see Chapter 2, section titled 'Anger, Humor, Wit'). This invective, in his eyes at least, is clearly the most insulting one that he could use to express his utter contempt for a brahmin. He also often displays a deeply ingrained sense of scorn towards women, which perhaps is that of a man of his time, and which is possibly not stated so explicitly elsewhere except on certain occasions (e.g. in the Cittar poetry, but in a different way; see Chapter 2, section titled 'KāḼamēkam's Values and Worldview'). However, he did seem to greatly appreciate the company of devadasis and prostitutes, but never mentions a wife, a family,[27] or even teachers.[28] Either he did not have any or else he was a particularly private person.

But I digress. Perhaps the most solid (and explicit) historical clue that KāḼamēkam leaves us is the mention of CāḼuva Tirumalai Rāyan (e.g. v. 6, 206, 209), a viceroy who ruled in lieu of the Vijayanagara kings in the Cōḽa country, approximately between 1453 and 1468 CE (Zvelebil 1974: 53). While establishing the

---

[26]To know more about the Cittars and their poetry, see Zvelebil 1973: 218–36.

[27]In a verse (6) begging Tirumalai Rāyan for financial support, KāḼamēkam states that he and his children had nothing but air to eat. And Puliyūr (2010: 7) believes this shows that the poet had children. This may also simply be a common topos for poets who seek to appeal to the patron's compassion.

[28]It is believed that Ñāna Varōtayan was his teacher. See Chapter 2, section titled 'Pride and Sensitivity'.

poet's dates, Kāḷamēkam's verses that mention this regent also show us that he sought patrons to support him as a poet, as did many of his counterparts and predecessors across the land in this long-established tradition.[29] His attacks on other poets clearly spring from an atmosphere of rivalry and insecurity, and the ensuing conflicts for obtaining the king's favour and patronage (see Chapter 2, section titled 'Pride and Sensitivity').

Apart from this king's court (or capital?), which he refers to as *tirumalai rāyaṉ varai* ('Tirumalai Rāyaṉ's place'[30]; e.g. v. 64 and 66) Kāḷamēkam also mentions many towns in the Tamil land, to which he seems to have travelled—possibly to visit places in view of undertaking pilgrimage and/or of seeking patronage—if his references to them are indeed evidence of travel (see Chapter 3, section titled 'A Pilgrim's Progress').[31]

[29]Classical Tamil poetry clearly indicates that many poets sought patronage to support themselves financially. See Shulman 1992 for more on the topic, and for a brief but pertinent discussion about poets and patrons, see Tschacher 2011: 7–8. Please note that the *Cittira maṭal*, another one of Kāḷamēkam's works, has as its hero TeyvaṅkaḷPerumāḷ, a chieftain from the town of Pāvai in the Cōḻa land and a patron of the poet (Cuntaraṉār 1978: 6).

[30]*Varai* means 'boundary' but also 'mountain'. Cāmiṉātaiyar (1991 [1938]: 132) identifies this place with the modern-day Tirumalairāyaṉ Paṭṭiṉam, which is supposed to have been submerged in sand due to Kāḷamēkam's curse.

[31]Popular discussions (often held online, e.g. https://groups. google.com/g/vallamai/c/-zBKityEkR8/m/MruzSKShajoJ; accessed 6 April 2023) suggest that Kāḷamēkam may have gone from one temple town to another, eaten there, and spent time with the devadasis belonging to those temples. This could be true since, for example, he mentions the names of the devadasis along with their towns, where important temples also happen to be located.

Apart from this, there is very little that we know for sure about Kāḷamēkam, although he lived barely a few centuries ago. He has become something of a mythical person, which has contributed to countless stories that speak of his various exploits. But his poetry, which I shall introduce now, does tell us about his character, values, feelings, and so forth.

Kāḷamēkam's Poetry

Kāḷamēkam was an extempore poet and therefore bore the title of *ācukavi* (see the elegiac verse quoted in the previous section). And although he has also composed the 'Tiruvāṉaikkā ulā', a poem in the *ulā* 'short genre'[32] dedicated to Śiva as the main deity of the Tiruvāṉaikkā temple-town, and a few other works,[33] Kāḷamēkam is essentially known for his self-contained verses, known as *taṉippāṭal* in Tamil,[34] of which there are approximately 200.[35] Speaking of

[32]This genre describes women falling in love at first sight with a victorious hero who comes in procession.

[33]Apart from this, works such as *Caracuvati mālai, Parapiramma viḷakkam* and *Cittira maṭal* have been attributed to Kāḷamēkam, of which only the last seems to have survived.

[34]For a pertinent introduction to this type of verses, see Rao and Shulman 1998: 1–25

[35]Aruṇācalam (2005 [1969]: 367) indicates that Tillaiyampūr Cantiracēkara Kavirāca Paṇṭitar's 1878 edition of Kāḷamēkam's self-contained verses has gathered 187 verses by Kāḷamēkam and that by 1908, that number had grown to 204 in Mu. Rā. Kantacāi Kavirāyar's edition. He believes that many verses sung by different poets over many centuries have perhaps been attributed to Kāḷamēkam if they happened to be similar in style or contents. And it is difficult to tell them apart, especially if they happened to be intentional pastiches. Please note that the *Mañcari*

independent verses, especially in the south Indian context, Velcheru Narayana Rao and David Shulman (1998: 7) point out that

> . . . a *cāṭu* is not really an isolated verse, even if it appears as such. It is an integral part of a system of communicated and shared knowledge, often with strong intertextual connections and interactive relationships between these apparently independent verses. We are looking at a well-defined body of verses, many with associated stories and contexts, that has maintained itself as a coherent whole through oral communication from generation to generation among a specific group of people . . .

The same applies to Kāḷamēkam's verses, which not only speak to each other, but also interact with the past and contemporary poetic works, although the style, contents, and spirit of Kāḷamēkam's poetry can greatly differ from them. It is, of course, possible that some of the verses attributed to him are clever imitations or erroneous attributions, intentional or otherwise. As a matter of fact, it has been argued that some of the verses believed to be his were actually composed by another poet known for his sarcasm and bore it as his title, namely, Vacaikavi Āṇṭāṉ Kavirāyaṉ (eighteenth–nineteenth centuries?; see Tacarataṉ 1994: 29[36]) or even by a certain Taṇṭapāṇi Cuvāmikaḷ (Tacarataṉ 1994: 15).[37] While the metre of

---

quotes merely around ninety verses, and the *Caritai*, twenty-two. The modern editions, too, have different numbers of verses, but that could be due to editorial choices and censorship, as we shall see later.

[36]Tacarataṉ (1994: 38) also points out that Āṇṭāṉ was a 'Vaiṣṇava brahmin of the Cikkalār lineage or a Ciccili Cōḻiyaṉ'.

[37]This argument has been made by Tacarataṉ in his 1994 book dedicated to this other, much less known poet. Tacarataṉ

the contested verses can sometimes help us determine the authenticity of the authorship claims, it is not a foolproof method: Kāḷamēkam predominantly (but not exclusively) uses the *veṇpā* metre, and many of the verses found only in Śrītaraṉ's (2013) edition—for example, the verse *cellārum poḻil* (v. 69) or *oru māṭum* (v.72)—are not *veṇpā*s. That could potentially mean that they were not authored by Kāḷamēkam, but there is no guarantee of that, since he occasionally uses other metres as well. Since no scholar has, to my knowledge, produced a critical edition, it is difficult to tell apart the genuine verses from the fake ones, a task that is beyond the scope of this book. And vice versa, the issue of authorship has been exacerbated— possibly over the centuries, but definitely in the modern times—by the editorial choice that consisted in leaving out some of this poet's verses likely out of a sense of modesty due to the explicit nature of the contents. For example, Puliyūr (2010) and Śrītaraṉ (2013) omit two verses (*pala kāl* and *iṭṭiṭṭu* that create a double entendre between a basket and female genitals, and a raft and a woman's pubic region, respectively). Both verses are *veṇpā*s, and very much sound like Kāḷamēkam's, reminding one of his other *cilēṭai* verses, such as *pāra talai* (v. 58) that compares a coconut tree and a prostitute. These would have been lost had Piḷḷai (2020 [2006]) not included them in his anthology, just as many others verses probably already have vanished from collective memory. Indeed, the verse *pāra talai* is left out even by Śrītaraṉ, perhaps for very similar reasons, although he has a few verses that neither of

---

(1994: 14–15) believes that both Kāḷamēkam's and Kavirāyaṉ's verses have sometimes been attributed to the other by mistake.

the other two editors have incorporated (e.g. the two mentioned above).[38] As far as this book is concerned, I have used the widely available Puliyūr's 2010 edition as the basis, to which I have added variants and other verses from Piḷḷai (2020 [2006]) and Śrītaraṉ (2013) and have indicated them accordingly. Now that we have briefly touched upon the issues of authorship and editions, let us go back to Kāḷamēkam and his self-contained verses per se.

Even though other poets, such as Oppilāmaṇi (1375–1425 CE according to Zvelebil 1974: 53), have produced *taṉippāṭals*, very few are considered by scholars to be as good as Kāḷamēkam, even accounting for tastes. Aruṇācalam (2005 [1969]: 31) suggests that apart from our poet, it is only the twin-poets (*iraṭṭai pulavar*) in the century preceding Kāḷamēkam who produced good literary verses in the *taṉippāṭal* genre. Although this might be true, I also agree with Zvelebil (1974: 53) that while some of our poet's verses are 'witty and sharp, some of them [are] mere word juggleries, or, at best, palindromes and acrostics',[39] as we shall see. As mentioned earlier, traditional stories

---

[38]Apart from that, the *Caritai* (p. 53) also contains verses attributed to Kāḷamēkam that are not found elsewhere (e.g. v. 186–87). It is likely that some other earlier publications, which I have not been able to access, have a different set of additions as well. Cāminātaiyar (in Vaittiyanātaṉ 1986: 114) quotes one such verse that has not been published, at least not till he died. As said earlier, it is beyond the scope of this book to dive into this question. Hopefully, someday, we will have critical editions of all these Tamil poets, and such authorship issues can be clarified with more ease and confidence.

[39]Zvelebil (1974: 53) points out that these are very common in the post-Māgha Sanskrit poetry.

tell us that some of his verses were composed under the life-threatening *yamakaṇṭam* conditions, in which a poet could be punished with death if he breaks the agreed rules and does not manage to produce verses as per the demands. And this may explain why Kāḷamēkam has composed many *camicai* and *cilēṭai* verses (Aruṇācalam 2005 [1969]: 38), of which we shall see examples at present.

But before we do so, it is worth mentioning at the very outset that Kāḷamēkam's poetry is usually not philosophical or deep in nature, not even his 'bhakti' verses. He stays away from abstract notions and composes about all the things and people that he sees and/or interacts with. His poetry is in that sense very worldly, beautiful in its earthiness, but also rendered striking by his wordsmithery. However, he was also capable of composing on lofty subjects (e.g. poems on gods), just as he was able to deal with trivial themes and people (e.g. a comparison between a palm-leaf manuscript and a gun in v. 66). Thus, gods, kings,[40] vegetable vendors (e.g. v. 178), animals, and insentient entities all made up the subjects who peopled his poetic corpus.

Some of the astounding verses produced by him contain *cilēṭai* and/or *yamaka*,[41] while some (e.g. 72; see below) are *cittirakavis*—'metrical composition[s] fitted into fanciful figures' (MTL)—which Zvelebil (1974:

---

[40]For example, he praises the generosity of the chief of the Āmūr town (v. 206), Tirumalai Rāyaṉ, sometimes even praising his sword (v. 8) in order to flatter him and ingratiate himself to him.

[41]'Repetition, in a stanza, with changes of meaning sometimes effected by changes in the division of words' MTL; s.v. *yamakam*.

53) believes he produced 'under the decisive impact of Sanskritic prosody and rhetoric'. Let me present here a few verses by the poet to give the reader a taste of his exquisite (and less exquisite) poetry, although some of them deserve to be heard rather than read, like the following one. Since it is a language-dependent verse, I present the first one here in the written form (both in the Tamil script for the visual aspect, and the transliterated version) to allow the reader to perceive the alliteration visually, for want of a better option:

தாதித் தூதோதீது தத்தை தூதோதாது
தூதிதூ தொத்தி தத் தூதிதே – தாதொத்த
துத்தித் தாதேது தித்தித்தேத் தொத்தீது
தித்தித் தோதித் திதி.

tātīt tūtōtītu tattai tūtōtātu
tūtitū totti tat tūtatē − tātotta
tuttitat tātētu tittittēt tottītu
tittit tatōtit titi. 72

An *ōreḻuttup pāṭṭu*, a verse solely composed with the consonant *t*, is not just a tongue-twister, but also considered a type of *cittirakavi* by the *Yāpparuṅkalam*, an eleventh-century work on Tamil prosody, as rightly shown by Mātavaṉ (1983: 146). Splitting the words in the following way, we obtain one way of reading this challenging verse, based on Puliyūr's interpretation (2010: 48):

tātīt tūtō ītu; tattai tūt' ōtātu;
tūti tūt' ottittat tūt'atē − tāt'otta
tutti tattātē tutittut − tēt tot ītu
tittittat' ōtit titi. 96

As for the maid-servant's errand, it is faulty;
the parakeet will not utter the message;

> The female messenger's errand will come too late;
> [Also] bad is worshipping god and following [him].
>
> In such a way that pollen-like spots do not spread
>   [all over the body],
> Keep reciting [instead] the sweet [name of the lover]!

The different ways of splitting and attributing slightly varied meanings to the same words can also produce a somewhat nuanced meaning of the verse. The following is based on Śrītaraṉ's (2013: 192–3) interpretation:

> *tātīt tūtō tītu; tattai tūt' ōtātu;*
> *tūti tūt' ottittat tūt'atē − tāt'otta*
> *tutti tattātē tutittut tētt' ott' ītu*
> *tittittat' ōtit titi.*
>
> As for the maid-servant's errand, it is faulty;
> the parakeet will not utter the message;
> Oh messenger, your message-taking will be suitable!
> Worshipping and comforting [him],
> Speaking what is sweet, protect [me]!

The mild difference in the meaning begins at line 3. Thus, we can see that just because the poet's focus is on the sounds does not mean that the contents suffer: as a matter of fact, he has produced an *akam*-like verse which would have made any Caṅkam poet proud. The desperate girl in love thinks of ways to contact her beloved and rules out a few/all options. This verse has been found to be so impressive that a modified version was used in a Tamil film of the 1960s.[42]

---

[42]The lyricist of the Tamil film *Vāṉampāṭi* (1963), the eminent poet Kaṇṇatācaṉ (1927–81), adapted this verse in the following way, although its meaning remains largely unchanged:

Kāḷamēkam was also famous for composing *śleṣa* verses that can be interpreted in more ways than one, often in two radically different ways, depending on each verse. While we will explore many verses of this type later, let me present one here, which can be read as an invocation to Śiva or Viṣṇu:

cāraṅka pāṇiyā rañcacakkarattar kañcaṉaimuṉ
ōraṅkaṅ koyta ukirvāḷar pāreṅkum
ēttiṭumai yāka riṉitā yivarummaik
kāttiṭuva reppōtum kāṇ. 208

Given above is the metrically split verse. Let us now see how to split the words to derive different interpretations:

Śiva

cāraṅkapāṇiyār añcu akkarattar kañcaṉai muṉ
ōraṅkam koyta ukirvāḷar pār eṅkum
ēttiṭ' umaiyākar iṉitāy ivar ummaik
kāttiṭuvar eppōtum kāṇ.

He with a deer in hand; he of the five syllables;
He whose nails previously plucked out a limb of the lotus [-born]
    Brahmā;

---

tāti tūtu tūtu tattum tattai collātu/ tūti tūtu ottittatu tūtu cellātu/ tētu tittit
tottu tūtu teyvam varātu - iṅku tutti tattum tattai vāḷa tittittatōtu.

And he glosses this (and through that, explains Kāḷamēkam's verse itself) in the following way:

aṭimait tūtu payaṉ paṭātu kiḷikaḷ pēcātu/ aṉput tōḷi tūtu ceṉrāl viraivil cellātu/
teyvattaiyē toḷutu niṉrāl payaṉ irukkātu/ iḷam tēmal koṇṭa kaṉṉi vāḷa iṉiyatu kūru

'A message [sent through] a servant will not be of use; parakeets will not speak; if a beloved female friend goes with a message, she will not go quickly; there will not be any use if one does nothing but worship God; say something sweet so that the young maiden with yellow spots lives!'

Please note that yellow/golden spots indicate love sickness.

He who has Umā on his body whom the whole world praises;
He will always protect you!

Viṣṇu

cāraṅkapāṇiyār; am cakkarattar; kañcaṉai muṉ
ōr aṅkam koyta ukir vāḷar; pār eṅkum
ēttiṭu maiyākar iṉitāy ivar ummaik
kāttiṭuvar eppōtum kāṉ.

He with the Śārṅga [bow] in hand; he with the beautiful discus;
He whose nails previously ripped Kaṃsa's singular body;
He whose dark body is praised by the whole world;
He will always protect you!

While it is not unusual for poets to compose such verses, we can say that Kāḷamēkam has definitely mastered the art of *śleṣa*. Let us look at another example in which the impact of the word-split is minimal on the meanings of verse as puns take over. In the following verse, as Puliyūr (2010: 72) rightly explains, a girl in love indulges in double entendre while chatting with her friends in order to avoid stating explicitly what her wishes are. To all intents and purposes, the verse seems to mean this:

nērr' irā vant'oruvaṉ nittiraiyil kaippiṭittāṉ
vērr' ūrāṉ eṉru viṭāy eṉrēṉ—ārriyē
kañci kuṭiy' eṉrāṉ. 'kaḷit tiṉru/kaḷitt' iṉru pōv' eṉrēṉ
vañciyarē ceṉrāṉ maraintu. 108

Last night, a man held my hands in my sleep.
Thinking that he was from another town, I said, 'Thirst!'
He said, 'Cool the gruel and drink it!'
I said, 'Eat *kaḷi*[43] before leaving!'
        O pretty girls, he vanished away!

[43]This is a dish made with either millet flour or with black gram combined with rice and jaggery. See MTL, s.v. *kaḷi*.

The girl seems to be reporting an interaction in her dream between a stranger who mocks the girl who was perhaps offering him hospitality, and she retorts in kind. However, the veiled message is that, albeit in a dream, the girl mistakenly takes the man who makes advances to her to be a stranger, only to realise that he is her beloved. She then invites him to spend some pleasant time with her before he leaves homes:

> Last night, a man held my hands in [my] sleep.
> Thinking that he was from another town, I said 'Let go!'
> Pacifying [me], he said, 'Kāñci is my town!'
> I said, 'Enjoy yourself before leaving!'
>   O pretty girls, he vanished away!

It is another verse with an *akam* motif, and one that was wholeheartedly adopted by the bhakti poets: the girl seems bereft, for she does not get to rejoice in the company of her beloved (in this case, Śiva-Ekāmbaranātha who dwells in Kāñci according to Puliyūr 2010: 72) even in her dream. The double entendre is produced by the pun on the words *kañci* ('Kāñci' city/'gruel') and *kuṭi* ('town'/'drink'), as well as the way the expression *kaḷit tinṟu* is split (*kaḷit tinṟu* 'having eaten *kaḷi*', or *kaḷitt' inṟu* 'enjoying today'). Kāḷ amēkam thus adds his touch (and a bit of humour) to whatever type of poem he composes.

Perhaps less engaging, at least to my taste, are Kāḷamēkam's other type of *śleṣa* verses—in which polysemy, homonyms, and different word splits allow us to have multiple verses in one (e.g. Śiva and the pumpkin, the gun and the palm-leaf manuscript, and so forth). I add another example here—which is similar to the verse quoted above (v. 208) and which could be read as either referring to Śīva or to Viṣṇu—because we find a number of verses by Kāḷamēkam that are similar to this, as the editorial comments suggest that he composed them to fit the criterion set by someone, possibly a rival. The following one is a three-in-one kind of a verse that speaks of the rainbow, Viṣṇu, or the betel leaf.

nīri luḷatā niṟampaccai yāṟṟiruvṟl
pāriṟ pakaitīrkkum pānmaiyāl – cārumaṉuṗ
palviṉaiyai māṟṟutalāṟ pārīr peruvāṉa
vilviṇṭu nērveṟ ṟilai. 67

Look! It is the great rainbow, Viṣṇu, and fine betel leaves
   [respectively] due to
   1) [the rainbow] coming into existence due to water; [its]
       colours being fresh;
       [its] beauty;
       [its] nature of ending enmity (= scarcity) in the world;
       [its] changing the manifold *karman* of the humans based on
       [the earth];
   2) [Viṣṇu's] lying on the water; [His] green hue; [the presence
       of] Śrī;
       [His] nature of ending enmity in the world;
       [His] changing the manifold *karman* of Manu who
       depended on [Him];
   3) [the betel-leaf] appearing in water; [its] colour being green;
       [its] nature of ending enmity in the world due to [its]
       auspiciousness;
       [its] changing the manifold [health] troubles of the humans
       based on [the earth].

If we follow the order in which Puliyūr (2010: 44) reads it, we notice that the poet begins by giving a brief description of the rainbow: it owes its existence to water in the form of rain drops, its colours are refreshing, and it is beautiful; being a harbinger of the rains, it brings about—or at least announces—an end to scarcity and thereby changes the fortune of the humans in their favour. The same set of epithets are then applied to Viṣṇu: he lies on the water, which is a reference to his reclining on the ocean of milk; he is of a greenish hue, and he bears his spouse Śrī on his chest at all times; he puts a stop to enmity between warring humans in this world, often by appearing here himself, and finally, he blessed Manu, the progenitor of the humans, by removing his *karman*. Kāḷamēkam allows the same sentences to also define betel leaf: it grows by the waterbodies; it is green; and as it is considered propitious and used on auspicious occasions, it removes negative elements, such as enmity between the people; and finally, because of its medicinal properties, it cures humans of their various ailments. While such verses definitely show Kāḷamēkam's undoubtable mastery over both the Tamil language and poetics, they do tend to become redundant as he seems to stick to this formula of success and produces many of them, as mentioned earlier. It makes us wonder if the story of the *yamakaṇṭam* was true after all, or if he simply enjoyed a challenge of this kind.

Apart from *śleṣas*, Kāḷamēkam has also composed riddle-like verses. One of the well-known *akam* topos is that of exorcising a young lovelorn girl: when a mother becomes worried after spotting signs of love and pining in her daughter and (mis)interprets them as signs of possession by some deity (usually Muruku), she calls in the priest (*vēlaṉ*) to perform a special ritual to exorcise her (*veṟiyāṭṭu*).[44] Here is a short verse from

---

[44]The same topos was adapted by the bhakti poets as well, in which the girl's beloved is God Himself, and a rather enlightened

the *Aiṅkuṟunūṟu* (241), a collection of *akam* verses from the Caṅkam period:

nam uṟu tuyaram nōkki, aṉṉai
vēlaṉ tantāḷāyiṉ, a- vēlaṉ
veṟi kamaḻ nāṭaṉ kēṉmai
aṟiyumō tilla, ceṟi eyiṟṟōyē?

O lady with tightly-set teeth!
If Mother summons the Vēlaṉ-priest seeing our distress,
will that Vēlaṉ-priest know of [y/our[45]] friendship
    with the man from the fragrant land, *tilla?*

This simple verse brims with irony because the girls know the truth about the cause of the 'possession' (the lover), which the mother or the priest do not. Let us now see how Kāḷamēkam uses that same topos:

mum nāṉkil oṉṟu uṭaiyāṉ munnāṉkil oṉṟu eṭuttu
munnāṉkil oṉṟiṉ mēl mōtiṉāṉ munnāṉkil
oṉṟ' ariruntāl ākumō o o maṭamayilē
aṉṟu aṇaintāṉ vārāviṭṭāl. 187

[Kāma] with one of the twelve [zodiac signs as his banner]
  (the fish)
picked up an[other] of the twelve [signs] (the arrow),
and smit an[other] of the twelve (the virgin)!
Will it do to cut one of the twelve (a goat), alas, O young peahen!
    If he who embraced [me] that day does not come?

Very much as in the *akam* verse quoted above, the mother is trying to sacrifice a goat to cure her 'possessed' daughter, while the girl herself ruefully

---

soothsayer (instead of a simple exorcist), who appears to solve the problem. See, for example, Tirumaṅkai Āḻvār's *Ciṟiya Tirumaṭal.*

[45]This is one of the verses in which it is not clear whether it is the heroine or her friend who is speaking.

remarks that unless her beloved appears, the animal sacrifice is not going to be very effective. While there is nothing innovative about the topic, what sets this verse apart is the way Kāḷamēkam uses the different signs of the zodiac (without explicitly naming them) to convey his desired meaning.[46]

Let us now read another impressive riddle of a verse, which showcases the poet's way with words, as he lists individual syllables at the beginning, which at first glance do not make any sense:

> *cō kā mā ē vā tā collin̠ man̠ai kūṭṭi, umai*
> *pāk'ārnta tillaip paramēcar − vākāy*
> *tarittār, erittār, tar̠ittār, utaittār*
> *urittār kan̠ai paṭaittār ūrkku.* 21

[By] adding *man̠* to the words *cō, kā, mā, ē, vā, tā,*
the supreme lord in Tillai, half of whose [body] belongs to Umā,
    wore [*Cōman̠*, the moon] prettily,
    burnt [*Kāman̠*, the love-god],
    cut down [*māman̠*, his father-in-law Dakṣa],
    kicked [*Ēman̠*, Yama, the god of death],
    skinned [*vāman̠* a male elephant],
    turned [*tāman̠*, Dāmodara-Kr̥ṣṇa] into an arrow
        [to destroy] the [three] cities![47]

---

[46]Perhaps worthy of note is his use of the kind of astrology that was not known during the Caṅkam period.

[47]Śiva's wife occupies the left half of his body; he wears the moon on his locks; he burnt the love-god who tried to disturb his penance; he killed his father-in-law Dakṣa, due to whom his wife had killed herself; he kicked the god of death in order to protect Mārkaṇḍeya, a devotee of his; he also killed an elephant-demon, and he turned Kr̥ṣṇa (an incarnation of Viṣṇu) into an arrow to destroy the three cities that belonged to Asuras.

In the very first line, the poet gives the reading method ('Adding *man* to the words *cō*, *kā*, *mā*, *ē*, *vā*, *tā*'). In the second, he gives the agent (Śiva), and in the following lines, he lists verbs of action without giving their objects, which the reader is supposed to find out from the words that are obtained by suffixing *man* to the list of syllables, in the right order. Although the meanings are not uncommon, the way in which the poet presents the contents is masterly. Please note that while he lists a few of Śiva's exploits, he does not exactly make it an overt praise poem or a prayer.

Kāḷamēkam also experimented with other genres, like bhakti verses (see Chapter 3) and perhaps less frequently, with minor Tamil genres, like the *ulā* (see fn 32), in which women watch a procession headed by a victorious hero and fall in love with him. The following is a verse in which a girl falls in love with Rāma, an uncommon choice for such a genre, since he is, the poet reminds us, well-known for his loyalty towards his wife, although the verse is reminiscent of Kampaṉ's in his *Irāmāvatāram* (*Ulāviyaṟpaṭalam*), as he describes Rāma walking down the lanes of Mithilā, leaving the lovelorn women of that city to suffer from lovesickness:

> *ōr oru mā oṉru mā oṉpatu māviṉ kalaiyai*
> *īr oru mā mummāvukk' īntatē-pār aṟiyap*
> *poṉ māṉiṉ piṉ pōṉa pūmaṅkaiy āḷvārai*
> *kaṉmāviṉ vīti varak kaṇṭu. 166*

Kāḷamēkam introduces a pun based on the syllable-word *mā* here, especially in the first two lines: the first *mā* is an epithet of goddess Śrī-Lakṣmī, while the other '*mā*' refers to the fraction 1/20th.

TABLE 1: Explanation of the Syllable *mā* in v. 166.

onru mā	1 *mā*	= ten *mās*
onpatu mā	9 *mās*	= ½ = *arai*
īr oru mā	2 *mās*	= 5 *mās*
mummā	3 *mās*	= ¼ = *kāl*

While *arai* and *kāl* mean 'half' and 'quarter', respectively, in this context, they are also homonyms for body parts, namely, 'waist' and 'leg, foot', respectively. And this gives the following meaning to the verse:

Seeing the Lord of the Flower-Lady
    —who went after the golden deer
    as the [whole] world knows—
come in the street thanks to [her good] deeds,
a singular Lakṣmī[-like girl] gave the waist belt to [her] feet!

The slipping-off of ornaments and even clothes due to an all-consuming passion or pining that causes a girl to become emaciated instantly (especially at the levels of the waist and the wrists) is a common topos in Indian literature, including in the Caṅkam literature.[48] The *Meypāṭṭiyal* (2.262) from the *Tolkāppiyam*, the oldest extant Tamil grammar (early first millennium), has a passage that describes such symptoms in the lovelorn woman as the loosening of the hair, the loss of an earring, her tightening of the bracelets that risk slipping down, and so forth. Kāḷamēkam uses this

---

[48]For example, in *Aiṅkurunūru* 2.20, the heroine laments that '[By] thinking of the man from the town (...) my bright, pretty bracelets will slip off my wrists!' (*ūranai uḷḷi en/ irai ēr el vaḷai nekiḻpu ōṭummē*).

topos; but what stands out in his verse is his pun on the syllable *mā* and the riddles that it creates, which is truly his trademark. He also uses a mild form of irony, as the girl falls in love with someone known for his single-minded devotedness to his wife Sītā: it is not a *coup de foudre* that is likely to have a happy ending, although she is herself described as Lakṣmī, whose avatāra Sītā was. The girl could be Sītā herself—if the reference to Rāma's notorious chasing of the golden deer and what it means vis-à-vis his love for his wife were not hinted at by the poet.

As we have seen, the poet has composed many verses based on puns, *śleṣa*s and so forth. He was a master wordsmith, who could bandy with words, and twist and bend them to fit metrical requirements as well. It is perhaps also worth mentioning here that some of Kāḷamēkam's verses can yield more than one interpretation which he clearly did not intend, as later scholars understand his words as well as they can in the absence of an old, definitive commentary (if at all such a thing exists!). Let us look at an example:

vāli maṭintatuvum val arakkar paṭṭatuvum
kōla muṭi mannar kuṟaintatuvum – cāla
matiy uṭaiya nūrr' oruvar māṇṭatuvum aiyō
cata vikarattāl vanta tālvu. 185

The perishing of Vālin;
the death of the mighty Rākṣasas;
The waning of kings with pretty crowns;
the perishing of the hundred and one people endowed with a
    [sound] mind:[49] *aiyō*!

[49]Since it follows immediately the mention of Vālin (by Rāma) and since it is the *Rāmāyaṇa* that mentions the Rākṣasas (more so than the *Mahābhārata*), the Rākṣasas alluded to here must be

[All this] is a degradation that came from *catavikaram*. 185

The verse deals with the different unfortunate events narrated in the twin epics—the *Rāmāyaṇa* and the *Mahābhārata*—which, the poet says, derive from *catavikaram*. Puliyūr (2010: 116–7) understands the word as *ca* + *ta* + *ikaram* = *ca* + *t* + *i* = *cati*, which could mean 'virtuous wife' (< Skt. *satī-*). Puliyūr even inverts the last two syllables of *vikaram* and turns it into *virakam* (<Skt. *viraha-*), 'separation of the virtuous wife'.[50] He thus believes our poet to be declaring that destruction follows when one tries to hurt or harm a virtuous wife or seeks to possess one by force: the deaths of Vālin and the Rākṣasas were (directly or indirectly) due to Rāvaṇa's abduction of Sītā, while the killing of the kings and the Kaurava brothers in the *Mahābhārata* was due to the extreme humiliation that they inflicted upon Draupadī when they tried to disrobe her publicly. However, Ceṅkai Potuvaṉ (n.p.)[51] understands *cati* as 'treachery' (*Dravidian Etymological Dictionary* 2323), and believes that this is a list of all

---

Rāvaṇa and his people. The decrease in the number of kings could be a generic reference to kings in general, or to the ones who died fighting in the *Mahābhārata* war. And the 101 people seem to refer to Duryodhana and his 99 siblings, to which Karṇa is added (Puliyūr 2010: 117). It is clear that the poet did not bother to take into consideration the fact that one of the hundred siblings was a woman, who obviously did not directly fight in the war nor die (although her husband Jayadratha did!).

[50]Śrītaraṉ (2013: 245) indicates that *cati virakam* is a variant reading.

[51]Apparently a Tamil scholar, Potuvaṉ has produced an e-text of Kāḷamēkam's verses (available online at https://ta.wikisource.org/wiki/ காளமேகப்_புலவர்_பாடல்கள்), to which he has added his comments. I have used this edition with extreme caution here.

the people that Māl-Nārāyaṇa killed by means of treachery. We thus see that Kāḷamēkam's verses are so rich that they can be interpreted in radically different ways even if he did not necessarily intend any *śleṣa* on those occasions.

CHAPTER TWO

Kāḷamēkam, the Man

THE SAMPLE POEMS quoted in Chapter 1 must have given an *aperçu* of Kāḷamēkam's wide repertoire of words and his command over metrics and poetics. But the poet's verses do more than that, for some of them allow us to know the poet more intimately: what was he like? What was his personality? What about his notorious temper? How did he perceive the world? What were his likes and dislikes? What did he believe in? While striving to seek answers to these questions, I will now focus on a few key topics that loudly proclaim who the poet was as a person, as a man.

Pride and Sensitivity

Kāḷamēkam's pride, which may have caused his legendary foul temper (cf. the following section), stands out among all his other attributes. However, these apparently negative aspects do not exclude a keen sense of humour on his part, which is palpable throughout his poetic corpus. Please note that anger, humour, and later on, devotion, are not necessarily mutually exclusive in Kāḷamēkam's self-contained verses, so there might be some overlap in the different parts of this book.

One of the first things that strikes us when reading Kālamēkam's verses is his overwhelming sense of pride, which he expresses without any inhibitions, as he never seems to shy away from praising himself—or perhaps, merely stating facts as far as he is concerned. Obviously 'fascinated with metapoetic issues that focus on the nature of the poetic and linguistic creativity' (Rao and Shulman 1998: 147) like many of his counterparts who composed independent verses, the poet speaks of his *āśukavitva*,[1] the lightning speed with which he claims to compose poetry, a sign of poetic genius, which fills him with untold self-esteem:

> Seven hundred, eight hundred [songs] before I say *im -*
> won't there be a thousand songs if I say *am*? 9

Along with speed, it seems that his capacity to produce good quality poetry is also something about which he greatly exaggerates. The poet continues,

If I sit, I just sit.
If I rise, I'm a great monsoon cloud/Kālamēkam, oh child! 9[2]

The person that he addresses, presumably a fellow poet, is dismissed disdainfully as being a mere child[3] before this great monsoon cloud, which—presumably when provoked—can rise to the sky, pour down words, and wash away petty rivals such as his current

---

[1]This is someone who composes extempore verses satisfying certain set conditions.

[2]*im ennum munnē eḻunūṟum, eṇṇūṟum/am enṟāl āyiram pāṭṭ' ākātō? cummā/*
iruntāl iruntēṉ eḻuntēṉē āyiṉ perum kālamēkam, piḷāy!

[3]Puliyūr (2010: 8–9), probably following the oral traditions, suggests that Kālamēkam is addressing a fellow poet, Atimatura Kavirāyar.

interlocutor. The activity of producing a flurry of words or poems has been compared to pouring clouds in the Indian context,[4] which is what Kālamēkam is alluding to here. Indeed, he is more explicit in v. 5, in which he extends the metaphor, while drawing a parallel between his poetry-making and the activities of the clouds.[5] In another verse, he gives further details in the form of precise examples of the types of works he could compose within a very short period of time:

> Five *nālikai*s[6] for a messenger poem;
> six *nālikai*s to utter a worded *cantamālai*;
> Seven *nālikai*s to utter a faultless *antāti*
> in a detailed way, so that they are [well-]assorted;
> Ten *nālikai*s for the *matal, kōvai*, [and so forth], which have
>   divisions;
> a whole day for a *parani*;
> a day or two to pronounce all the big *kāvya*s:
> I have [thus] declared victory! (…) 4[7]

[4]Even now, saying *aval polintut tallivittāl* (more literally, 'She has poured out showers'), for example, means that the person's words flowed uninterruptedly and even eloquently.

[5]*kali untiya katal upp' enru nal nūl katalin montu,/valiyum potiya varaiyinil kālvaitta, van kavitai moliyum pulavar manattē itittu, mulanki, minni,/poliyum patikkuk kavikāla mēkam purappattatē.*

'Like salt driven into the backwaters, the poet Monsoon Cloud/ has set forth in such a way that, drawing from the ocean of good books,/ and stepping onto the Potiya mountain where [streams] flow,/he thunders, roars, emits lightning, and pours in the hearts of the poets/ who utter hard verses!'

[6]A *nālikai* corresponds to twenty-four minutes.

[7]*tūt' añcu nālikaiyil, āru nālikai-tanil/ col canta-mālai collat/ tukal ilāv antātiy ēlu nālikai-tanir/ tokaipata viritt' uraikkap/ pātam cey matal kōvai patt unālikai-tanil/ paraniy oru nāl muluvatum/ pāra kāviyam elām ōr iru tinattilē/ pakarak koti-katti nēn . . .*

The poet probably lists these genres to clarify that as an *āśukavi*, he does not compose just any banal verses, but tackles genres that need both exceptional poetic skills—and for most poets—plenty of time as well, due to the required lengths of such works (although evidently not for Kāḷamēkam!). For example, Cayaṅkoṇṭār's *Kaliṅkattu Paraṇi* (twelfth century?), the first (and by far the most well-known) work in the *paraṇi* genre,[8] is composed of 800 verses. Based on Kāḷamēkam's claims, had he written that epic poem, he would have composed 1.8 verses per minute for twenty-four hours, or 3.6 verses per minute if by the word 'day' he meant the time from dawn to dusk. Interestingly, a verse challenging this hyperbolic claim figures in Piḷḷai's (2020 [2006]) edition, and has been attributed to Atimaturakavi, his rival:

> If three hundred and four hundred songs appear before
> you take a breath,
> wouldn't there be a thousand if you say 'done!'?
> What's [this] talk?
> O naïve poet Kāḷamēkam! Wrap up your fake poems![9]

Whether this verse was indeed composed by Atimaturakavi (who has not left behind any works) or not, it shows that poets did call other poets out for such hyperbolic claims, thus attesting to the bitter rivalry among them.

Self-praise in Kāḷamēkam is often accompanied by criticism and mockery of other poets, whether past

---

[8]A *paraṇi* is 'a poem about a hero who destroyed 1000 elephants in war' (MTL).

[9]*mūccu viṭu munnē munnūṟu(m) nānūṟum/ āccut' enṟāl āyiram pāṭṭākātā? – pēcc' enna?*

veḷḷaik kavi kāḷamēkamē! ninnuṭaiya/ kaḷḷak kavikkaṭaiyaik kaṭṭu!

or contemporary, great or small. Let us begin with a verse in which our poet shows his irritation at the master poet Kampan's decision to shorten the length of a vowel to suit the metrical needs of his verse:

nārāyaṇaṉai narāyaṇaṉ eṉṟē kampaṉ
ōrāmal coṉṉa uṟutiyāl nērāka
vār eṉṟāl var eṉpēṉ vāḷeṉṟāl vaḷeṉpēṉ
kār eṉṟāl kar eṉpēṉ nāṉ. 204.

Due to the certainty of Kampan, who addressed Nārāyaṇa
As Nārāyaṇa without paying attention,
I shall similarly say *var* for *vār*, *vaḷ* for *vāḷ*
And *kar* for *kār*.

This is a reference to v. 23 in the *Iraṇiyaṉ vatai paṭalam* in the *Yutta kāṇṭam* in Kampan's *Irāmāvatāram*, the most prominent retelling of the *Rāmāyaṇa* in Tamil. The *paṭalam*, which deals with the killing of Hiraṇyākṣa by Nārāyaṇa, has Prahlāda recite Nārāyaṇa's eight-syllabled mantra: *ōnamō narāyaṇāyav eṉṟ' uraitt' uḷam uruki* ... 'Uttering *ō[m] namō narāyaṇāya* and with a melting heart. . . .' As we can see, it is not just any syllable, but the first syllable of an extremely important word, *nārāyaṇa*—and that too embedded in a mantra, which ought not to be tampered with—which Kampan reduces to a short '*a*'. Kāḷamēkam belligerently declares that he would follow suit. While Kampan may have done this either not to disturb the metre and/or not to reveal the mantra so explicitly, our poet is not amused. Or is he? The editor of a *Irāmāvatāram* edition, Vai. Mu. Kōpālakiruṣṇamamāccāriyār (2011 [2006]: 87), quotes this verse by Kāḷamēkam and suggests that the poet says it for fun (*vēṭikkaikkāka*).[10]

---

[10]Heated online debates (e.g. https://groups.google.com/g/

Having criticized one of the most eminent Tamil poets, Kāḷamēkam is obviously not going to feel any reluctance about putting down other less formidable and more contemporary ones, individual rivals[11] or indeed groups of poets. In the following verse, he describes other poets as monkeys, by means of a pun made possible by the Sanskrit noun *kapi* ('monkey'), which can be pronounced as *kavi* ('poet') in Tamil:

> Where's the tail?
> Where's the elongated belly?
> Where are the two legs in the front?
> Where are the sunken eyes?
> O you poets abundantly praised by kings!
> You must be monkey kings (*kavi/pi-rāja*)![12]

Taking *kavirāja* as *kapirāja*, Kāḷamēkam hurls these insults at the other poets, who were probably patronized by kings. Is the poet annoyed that poor poetry is being produced, since he does speak of 'poets who utter hard verses' *val kavitai moḻiyum pulavar* (v. 5) elsewhere? Or that it is accepted and celebrated by people in power, despite being so very inferior to his own verses? Or is it their hostile or proud attitude

---

santhavasantham/c/5akKpc9Y9nI, accessed on 8 September 2023) suggest that this verse by Kāḷamēkam may have helped Vai. Mu. Kō. decide upon the variant *narāyaṇāya* rather than *nārāyaṇāya*, allegedly a case of hypercorrection that found its way into some publications like the *Irāmāvatāram* brought out by the Cennai Kampaṉ Kaḻakam. Being quoted by Kāḷamēkam also rules out the theory that this verse may have been an interpolation (and if it was, then it is a relatively old one).

[11]He also takes on individual poets, e.g. v. 3.

[12]*vāl eṅkē? nīṇṭa vayir' eṅkē? muṉ iraṇṭu/ kāl eṅkē? uṭkuḻinta kaṇ eṅkē? – cāla/ puvirāyar pōṟṟum pulavīrkāḷ! nīvir/ kavirāyar eṉr' irunta kāl!* (10).

that provokes him, whatever their actual poetic skills? Or is our poet simply jealous that his poetry should not be appreciated as it deserves to be? Whatever the cause, it seems that his pride in his own *kavitva* ('poetic skill') goes hand in hand with disdain for the other poets, as we can see once again in the following verse, in which abuse gives way to aggression that reaches alarming levels:

(...) I am Poet Kālamēkam who,
  thus chopping off the ears of,
  horsewhipping,
  boxing the ears of
    the fraudulent versifying poets,
      who commit transgressions that always abound in confusion
        before the great Tirumalairāyan of lasting fame,
        a descendant of the cooling moon,
  fit them with a cruel bridle along with a victorious saddle,
  and climb upon them! [13]

In this verse, Kālamēkam compares the poets from Tirumalairāyan's court to unbroken-in horses, and promises terrible violence in the process of taming them, reminding us of the kind of violence that poetic rivals allegedly had to endure in the Tamil land.[14]

---

[13] *. . . cītam ceyum tiṅkaḷ marapināṉ nīṭu pukaḻ/ ceyya tirumalarāyaṉmuṉ/ cīṟu-māṟ' eṉrum miku tāṟumāṟukaḷ cey/ tiruṭṭu kavi pulavarai/ kāt' aṅk' aṟuttu, cavukk'iṭṭ' aṭittu,/ katuppil puṭaittu, veṟṟi/ kallaṇaiyiṉoṭu koṭiya kaṭivāḷam iṭṭ' ēṟu/ kavi kālamēkam nāṉē.* 4

[14]This is reminiscent of the extreme punishments supposedly meted out at the Jains after they lost their debates with the Śaiva saints, as narrated in the Śaiva hagiographic text, the *Periya Purāṇam* (*inter alia*). In the stories on (and around) Tamil saints or poets, it is common to come across physical mutilation or other such form of chastisement (and/or humiliation) of the losing rivals, something that both parties may have agreed to

Once again, we notice that for our poet, the other side of the coin of self-praise is often the belittling of the other poets. The laudatory words directed at the king, 'the great Tirumalairāyan of a lasting fame, a descendant of the cooling moon' points at the poet's vying for royal patronage.

One of the few poets whom Kālamēkam respects and has good words for is someone called Ñāna Varōtayan, whom Aruṇācalam (1944: 30) claims was his teacher, without backing it up with any data.[15] In the following verse, we come across one of the rare instances in which Kālamēkam praises a fellow poet:

O Ñāna Varōtayan!
The forty-nine [Caṅkam poets] are not there to learn properly
    your songs in clear, ripe Tamil
and counter-compose [verses] aplenty!
The [Pāṇdya] king
    —who perceives chaff among the sweet Tamil [verses] and
        casts it off—
is not there!
There is no [Caṅkam] plank to climb upon!
How could you go to Madurai?[16]

Presuming that Kālamēkam's words are not sarcastic

---

in the pre-challenge agreement. For example, it is believed that Villiputtūrār, the composer of the Tamil *Mahābhārata*, went around challenging the poets of his times threatening to cut off their ears of the losers.

[15]It is not clear whether this Ñāna Varōtayan (early fifteenth century) is the same as the disciple of Kacciyappar, who wrote the *Kantapurāṇam* in Tamil. The former composed the *Upatēcakaṇṭam*, a sequel to this *Kantapurāṇam* (Shulman 1980: 32).

[16]*mutirat tamil teri nin pāṭal tannai muṟaiy aṟintē/ etir okkak kōppataṟk' ēl ēlu pēr illai! in tamilin/ patarait terint' eri kōv illaiy! ēṟap palakaiy illai!/ maturaikku nī cenṟat' evvāṟu? ñāna varōtayanē!* 209

(as he generally does not bother to mince his words or hide his contempt), his praise is extreme, since comparing another poet favourably with the Caṅkam poets—who are the yardstick with which to measure the quality of poetry among the Tamils, and whom many try to emulate, including Kāḷamēkam—is no mean praise.

Except on a few such occasions, we mostly only get to witness Kāḷamēkam's sense of pride in himself, which is probably one of the main reasons that make him either lose his temper or resort to mockery. Thus, the poet's foul temper—which leads to some unrestrained tongue-lashing—and his sense of ridicule are palpable throughout his poetry, giving him a notoriety that has survived him by many centuries. What provokes him to a fit of anger or a peal of laughter also tells us about his personality, his likes and dislikes, his values and worldview. And that is what we are going to focus on now.

Many things upset our poet, and one main cause for his feeling anger, irritation, and despair is food. For, as mentioned earlier, Kāḷamēkam takes his food very seriously. Many are the situations in which he switches between loss of temper and good-natured humour. While he can shudder and joke about a bad experience when a hostess fails to serve a decent meal (see the following section), he is much less tolerant on other occasions, when his language becomes virulent. For example, when his co-eater's hair apparently unfolds onto his leaf-plate (or, according to the *Mañcari*, p. 263, his neighbour's hair falls onto his own food, causing him to shake his wet hair, thus sending some of the remnant food flying towards our poet's leaf-plate):

O Cōḻiya [Brahmin] with a forehead-tuft that became untied!
O you with dried grains of boiled rice on the lips!
O outcaste (*pulaiyā*)!
O owl from Tirukkuṭantai!
Dog!
Monkey!
  That some woman should have bothered to birth you![17]

Compared to the 'offence', this string of insulting epithets seems disproportionate, although clearly they come straight from his heart: except for the first, all his apostrophes are pejorative, mostly animal names. He also shows disgust for the appearance (and perhaps the lack of personal hygiene) of the other man by pointing out that he had not rinsed off his mouth properly, possibly for hours after eating (for the boiled rice had dried up on his lips). The *coup de grâce* is declaring the other man's existence an utter waste of energy on his mother's part. Puliyūr (2010: 119) records a variant that is equally insulting.[18] Apart from showing here that Kāḷamēkam does not wish anyone to come between him and his food, this verse also tells us a few things about the poet. In order to eat by the side of a Cōḻiya (brahmin), Kāḷamēkam would have had to be a brahmin too, for in his times, a *camapanti* ('commensality') that allowed people of all castes to sit

[17]*curukk' aviḻnta munkuṭumic cōḻiyā! cōrrup/ porukk' ularnta vāyā! pulaiyā! tirukkuṭantaik*
kōṭṭāṉē! nāyē! kuraṅkē! uṉaiy orutti/ pōṭṭāḻē vēlaiy arrup pōy! 189
[18]*corukkaviḻnta munkuṭumic cōḻiyā cōrrup/ porukk' ularnta vāyā pulaiyā - tirukkuṭantai*
nāyā nariyā! uṉ ṉāymukamum cēyvaṭivum/ tāyār tāṉ kaṇṭilaḻō tāṉ? 189

The variants can be translated as 'Dog from Tirukkuṭantai! Jackal! Did [your] mother not see your child's body and dog's face?'

together for food was probably not a common practice. The second thing that we notice is that Kālamēkam comes across as a casteist, although I am conscious that this claim could be interpreted as an anachronistic judgement based on today's values. But it is undeniable that he does insult another person using a caste-based invective: the word *pulaiyan* 'outcaste', which derives from *pulai* 'baseness, uncleanness, defilement, vice' (TL), is highly pejorative. Another thing that is worth noting is that, as mentioned in the first chapter, the Cōliya brahmins may have been looked down upon by the others: we may wonder if that is why Kālamēkam, not being one himself and therefore feeling superior socially, allows himself to lash out at the other man without restraint. However, as already mentioned in the previous chapter, Śrītaran (2013: 6) draws an entirely different conclusion, namely, that Kālamēkam was himself a Cōliya brahmin, not just because of his name, but also because of how free he feels to scold the other man. We cannot really find an answer to this question, since the latter argument cannot be very conclusive, not just because it is pure speculation, but also because Kālamēkam does not mind at all insulting most people around him, and in that sense, he does not discriminate against anyone.

Here is another example when food causes our poet to lose his temper: less insulting, but perhaps more resentful, is Kālamēkam's reaction to a delay in serving him food at a public feeding-house:

In the rest-house of Kāttān in Nākai surrounded by the
    roaring sea,
Rice is brought in when the sun sets.
By the time they are pounded and placed in the boiling water,
    the town goes to sleep.

[By] the time a ladleful of rice is served on the plantain leaf,
   the morning star will have risen![19]

While clearly displeased, Kāḷamēkam seems to keep his temper in check: he does not fully verbalize his anger in this particular case, for we do not find a list of invectives as in v. 189. He probably intends to put his anger to better use. So, while he merely seems to describe the events (with a bit of exaggeration), his pinning the exact location where such a disgraceful neglect occurred is perhaps intended to ruin the reputation of the institution, if not of the town, for all times to come. The technique seems to have borne fruit, since it has been suggested that once fed and apologized to, a pacified poet offers a different, positive interpretation of the same verse (*Mañcari*, p. 264; Piḷḷai 2020 [2006]: 131).[20]

[19]*kattu kaṭal cūḻ nākaik kāttāṉ-taṉ cattirattil/ attamikkum pōtil aricivarum – kutti*

ulaiyiliṭav ūraṭaṅkum ōr akappaiy aṉṉam/ ilaiyilaṭa veḷḷi yeḻum. 190

[20]Piḷḷai (2020 [2006]: 131) suggests the following interpretations (with my comments between parentheses): *attamikkum pōtil* = during famines (although the word *attam* at best means 'rough path, difficult course' TL); *ūr aṭaṅkum* = the townspeople will rejoice (although *aṭaṅku* means 'to settle, to subside, to be still' TL) since they will not be crying for food; *veḷḷi eḻum* 'Śukra/Venus has left' due to the brightness of the boiled rice. This alternative interpretation of certain words does not sound very convincing to me, but if we really could understand them the way the *Mañcari* and Piḷḷai suggest that we do, the end result would be the following:

In the rest-house of Kāttāṉ in Nākai surrounded by the roaring
   sea,
Rice is brought in times of difficulty. As it is pounded
and placed in the boiling water, the town settles down contentedly.

But why does Kālamēkam name and shame people in this way? Perhaps he is simply aiming at teaching the involved people a lesson by ruining their reputation or at reforming them by threatening to do so. In v. 214, for example, he scathingly criticizes a man who pretended not to be present at home to receive a guest, by pointing out how the Veḷḷāḷas (*vēḷān*) were known for their *viruntōmpal* ('welcoming and entertaining guests' TL). He declares that such a person is as good as non-existent by using the term *cākalānān* ('[as good as] dead'). In contrast, in v. 194, our poet praises a man who fed him well, as he gives the menu in detail, and in v. 193, he lauds Tiruppanantāḷ Paṭṭan, a food-donor. Since the poets have the capacity to immortalize a person through their words, his anger towards those who do not feed others properly could have simply been a blackmailing tactic to make people behave properly.

Food, thankfully (or unfortunately!), is not Kālamēkam's only trigger. Many other things can provoke him, especially ones that inconvenience and/or hurt him in some way. Especially in the latter case, his fury makes him utter sinister words. The *kiḷavi* for the following verse suggests that as he admired a child, the latter's mother—worried that her child might attract *dṛṣṭi-doṣam* (roughly, the 'evil eye')—cursed that

And as a ladleful of rice is served on a plantain leaf,
  Venus will leave [in shame]!

Poets cursing and taking back their curse are not infrequent. See, for example, Bhīmakavi's curse and countercurse (Rao and Shulman 1998: 12), although in that instance, the poet writes two different verses.

the poet be given (to Yama? Death?). The provoked Kāḷamēkam retaliates:

ennaik koṭuttāl irakkam uṉakk' uṇṭāmō?
vaṉṉak kamala muka valliyē! tuṉṉu matak
kāṭṭ' āṉaik kōṭṭu malaik kārikaiyē!
nī payatta kōṭṭāṉait tāṉē koṭu! 174

Will you feel compassion if you give me [to death]?
   O creeper with a colourful lotus face!
   O lady with mountain[-like breasts akin to the] tusks
      of a wild elephant with thick musth!
Give [to death] the owl that you begot instead!

He is wishing death upon an innocent child here, but clearly because he is offended that his own innocent gesture should bring upon him a curse.[21] Apart from the explicit counter-curse, the unspoken insult lies here, I think, in his lascivious description of presumably a married woman. It was probably his way of provoking that woman, unless she was one of the many devadasis that he dealt with. But of course, the *kiḷavi* could have coloured the way the verse was interpreted, and Kāḷamēkam might be reacting to a woman who insulted him for his inappropriate behaviour towards her. In fact, Piḷḷai (2020 [2006]: 135–6) interprets *ennaik koṭuttāl* as 'if I offer myself [to you]', which adds to the argument that he is flirting with her to her disapproval. Please note that Āṇṭāṉ Kavirāyaṉ seems to have sung a similar verse using identical words *uṉṉaik koṭuppēṉ*, which makes Tacaratan (1994: 31, 52) believe that this verse was

[21]The popular belief is that the child died after receiving Kāḷamēkam's curse, that its father begged to save it, to which the poet agreed, and the child was resuscitated.

not composed by Kāḷamēkam at all, although it very much sounds like our proud, irascible poet.

The only time that Kāḷamēkam swallows his pride—and perhaps keeps his short temper under control, surely despite provocation at a hostile royal court—is when he praises Tirumalairāyaṉ, the (potential?) patron, who is among the few who escape the extreme lashings of his tongue to a large extent. The chieftain (or his town), mentioned in thirteen verses—out of which eleven are laudatory—, also receives wholesome praise, the kind that even gods do not obtain from our poet:

> As the flood that is the glory of Bhīma-like mighty
>   Tirumalairāyaṉ expanded,
> Aja-Brahmā ran and entered Satyaloka from [his] lotus;
> [Viṣṇu-Trivikrama] with discus in hand grew from the
>   earth all the way up to the sky;
> [and] on Mount Kailāsa, Śiva wore the moon on his head
>   and checked
>   the depths [of the sea] with the staff that is the
>   northern mountain! 7.[22]

Unlike the bhakti poets who mostly swore single-minded, unswerving devotion to their god of choice and even scorned the very idea of singing in praise of humans,[23] Kāḷamēkam has no scruples about

---

[22]*vīmaṉ-eṉa vali mikunta tirumalairāyaṉ kīrtti veḷḷam poṅkat/
tāmaraiyiṉ ayaṉ ōṭic cattiyalōkam pukuntāṉ; caṅkapāṇi
pūmitoṭṭu vāṉamaṭṭum vaḷarntu niṉrāṉ; civaṉ kayilaip poruppil/
cōmaṉaiyum talaikk' aṇintu vaṭa varait taṇṭāl āḻañ cōtittāṉē.*

[23]Compare this with Tirumaḻicai Āḻvār's verse: 'I shall not sing of mankind with [my] tongue./ [My] songs [will] be on the red feet of the Lord of Vaikuṇṭha . . .' (*Nāṉmukaṉ Tiruvantāti* 75; *nāk koṇṭu māṉiṭam pāṭēṉ, ... vaikuntac/ celvaṉār cēv aṭimēl pāṭṭu.*).

lavishing hyperbolic praise upon a mortal chieftain, who seems to tower over the divine triad in this verse of his. When one has read his other verses, it is hard to imagine the poet being in earnest when lauding Tirumalairāyan, whom he is clearly trying to woo, presumably for monetary benefits.

Also uncharacteristic is our poet's expression of self-pity or his portraying himself in less than ideal light, which he does before the same chieftain. Indeed, in v. 6, Kālamēkam lists out all the signs of the extreme poverty that afflicts him: his rags have thousands of holes; he is perpetually hungry; he begs for food; he is emaciated; he always sheds tears; and his family and himself only have air for food. Along with that, he extols the king's generosity and begs him for riches. If the king grants him his wish, then he would become his 'faultless Supreme Being', clearly unlike the minor triad mentioned above. Indeed, as we shall see later, even the gods do not get such unadulterated homage from this poet, and this is one of the signs that Kālamēkam, while composing verses on gods, is not a bhakti poet—but that is something we shall deal with in Chapter 3.

We can thus clearly see that the poet does not mind swallowing his pride in order to please a potential patron. But that this praise is not the result of a deeply-rooted feeling of respect is visible from his words as his relations with the chieftain grow sour (or perhaps Tirumalairāyan never responded to Kālamēkam's overtures the way that the latter would have hoped for). Indeed, the poet curses (presumably) this chieftain's town, although he does not give any names:

> The town where widows' sons[24] live!
> The town that practises backbiting and deceit!
> The town where [people] stand and yell like bulls!
> Tomorrow itself,
>> turning pale,
>> bereft of rain clouds,
>> and getting angry,
>> may the sky pour down showers of sand.[25]

If indeed this verse-curse was directed at Tirumalairāyaṉ's town as Puliyūr's (2010: 10) *kiḻavi* suggests, Kāḷamēkam is careful not to name the place or the chieftain, or even throw around slurs as he is wont to do on other occasions. This is perhaps to avoid punishment at the hands of such a powerful ruler, for a curse is not exactly an insult, at least not always formulated as one, although some Tamil scholars (such as Tacaratan 1994: 12) take the view that *vacai* ('censure, satire') verses are identical with *cāpam* ('curse') verses.[26] However, 'widows' sons' is an ambiguous expression: it is hard to know if the poet refers to the fact that adult men have all died in the wars waged by the king (i.e. Tirumalairāyaṉ in this case); that the boys from his kingdom are brought up without the guiding presence of their fathers, and are

---

[24]Puliyūr (2010: 10) glosses this as *kolaikārar* ('murderers'), but this meaning is not attested in the MTL.

[25]*kōlar irukkum ūr! kōḷ karavu kaṟṟa ūr!/ kāḷaikaḷāy niṉṟu kataṟum ūr! nālaiyē*
viṇ māri aṟṟu, veḷuttu mika karuttu/ maṇ māri peyka inta vāṉ. 12

[26]Whether this curse concerns Tirumalairāyaṉ's town or not, this poem is reminiscent of the curse of Talakāḍu by Alamēlammā, a distraught, newly widowed royal wife who curses that place to be buried in sand, *inter alia* (Sivramkrishna 2005: 19–20).

hence unruly. Or, is this an insult to those people, since their mothers begot them well after their husbands died, in which case, the expression is synonymous with 'bastards'?

There is no such ambiguity in another verse, however, as the poet is more explicit while targeting his anger, naming the person who is the culprit in his eyes:

O father! Hara!
> Just as you ruined Kāma with the hot fire pouring from
> your eyes,
> destroy in half an instant the evil people
> in the place of Tirumalairāyaṉ who did undoable things,
> with a shower of sand![27]

We can observe here that he seeks divine intervention to bring about the ruin of this place, an uncommon practice for Kāḷamēkam, who prefers to deal with people directly by scolding, insulting, and/or laughing at them, as we have seen so far. This verse also shows us that while our poet remains cautious with the powers that be, he still shows courage by potentially inviting a ruler's wrath, which is perhaps why he needs a greater power to avenge him. While he does not do it often, we do catch him explicitly criticizing another ruler apparently for his brutish behaviour.[28] This is one

[27]*ceyyāta ceyta tirumalairāyaṉ varaiyil/ ayyā! araṉē! arai noṭiyil veyya talal*
kaṇ māriyāl mataṉai kaṭṭ' aḻittāṟ pōl tīyōr/ maṇ māriyāl aḻiya vāṭṭu. 13

[28]*cokkaṉ maturaiyil toṇṭarkku muṉṉ aviḻtta/ poyk kutirai caṇṭaikkup pōmatō?—mikka*
karacaraṇā! vantak karumpuṟattārkk' ellām/ arac' araṇā! māvali vāṇā! 211

of the rare instances in which our poet expresses an anger that is motivated by something beyond a selfish cause.

We have seen so far that Kāḷamēkam mostly bursts at the least provocation, curbing his tongue only on rare occasions. And we have also noticed that he reacts aggressively when he is personally affected by the other person. His relationship with others is, in fact, rather problematic, if not confrontational. And when he is not cursing them, he is laughing at them, as we shall see.

Anger, Humour, Wit

One of the most prevalent features found in Kāḷamēkam's poetry is his humour, not uncommon (albeit not overwhelmingly present) in Tamil literature. We find traces of it in the early poetry (e.g., *Kalittokai* 94), and the eleventh-century epic poetry by Cayaṅkoṇṭār, the *Kaliṅkattu Paraṇi*, is replete with it. In the section *Meypāṭṭiyal*, the *Tolkāppiyam* too seeks to define humour (*nakai*) by categorizing it into four groups:[29]

'Will the fake horses—that Cokkaṉ-Śiva let go in Madurai/ For the sake of [his] devotee—capable of going into battle?/ O you with big arms and legs! Is the ruler a protection for/ The hunters/Karumpurattār people? O Māvali Vāṇā!' The story of Śiva sending fake horses is the following: his devotee Vātavūrār builds a temple using the money meant for buying horses for the cavalry. When he is pressed by the king to produce the horses, Śiva decides to help by transforming wild foxes into horses and sends them the king. To read the whole story, see, for example, chapters 59 and 60 of the *Tiruvilaiyāṭal Purāṇam*.

[29]This is a slightly modified version of Indra Manuel's unpublished translation of the *Meypāṭṭiyal*.

ellal ilamai pētaimai maṭan̲ en̲r̲'
ul̲l̲a paṭṭa nakai nān̲k' en̲pa

Ridiculing, immaturity, ignorance, [and] credulity
Are the fourfold thought-out themes of laughter, they say.

While commentators—medieval and modern alike—discuss these categories, it will be pertinent to focus solely on *ell̲al* ('ridiculing') here, which is the most prevalent type of humour present in Kālamēkam's work, and its two aspects: the treatment of others while laughing at them and self-mockery. Medieval commentator Pērāciriyar mainly defines *ell̲al* as either ridiculing others or laughing when others ridicule oneself. However, Il̲ampūraṇar, another medieval commentator, mainly considers laughter as something that arises when ridiculing another, although he admits later on that it can also arise with respect to oneself. Modern commentator Cōma. Cuntara. Pāratiyār, however, believes that *ell̲al* is *il̲iyāccirippu*, 'laughter that does not belittle [another]'.[30] With this knowledge, let us now focus on the nature of Kālamēkam's humour, because mocking and deriding are second nature to him: does he hurt when using humour against the others? Does he allow himself to be laughed at by another, or at least laugh at himself?

We begin with a harmless joke about a slow horse, although it is likely that the poet was amusing himself at the expense of its owner:

mun̲n̲ē kaṭivāla(m) mūn̲r̲u pēr toṭṭ' il̲ukkap
pin̲n̲ēy irunt' iraṇṭu pēr tal̲l̲a − en̲n̲ēram

---

[30]I thank Indra Manuel for pointing these out to me in a personal communication (January 2023).

vētam pōm vāyāṉ vikaṭarāmaṉ kutirai
mātam pōṃ kāta vaḻi. 175

> As three people hold the bridle and pull it from the front,
> As two people push [the animal] from the back,
> The horse of Vikaṭarāmaṉ,
>   whose mouth was filled with the Vedas at all times,
> Will cover ten miles in a month!

We can see that although this is a *veṇpā* verse with the *etukai* rhymes at the right places, it is nothing out of the ordinary in terms of poetics; but the jest in its contents (which includes a hyperbolic statement) compensate for it. Since this verse is self-explanatory, let us move to another category, in which the joke can also be more explicitly made at someone else's expense. We already saw that Kāḷamēkam loves good food, which triggers all kinds of emotions in him and also tickles his sense of humour. In the following verse, when he is forced to eat food that is evidently not tasty, he feels the need to express that dreadful disappointment—downright torture even—in verse:

> If one sees it, one reaches Kailāsa!
> If one picks it up and eats it, it gives liberation!
> The pumpkin prepared by the anklet-footed lady from Koṇṭattūr
> Is meant for the celestials and for the lord (Śiva)![31]

This verse clearly comes from a place of suffering for a food-loving person: in the first two lines, the assault on the taste buds is implied, as is stated the lethal nature of the food upon earthlings, with the

---

[31]*kaṇṭakkāl kiṭṭum kayilāyam! vaikkoṇṭ'uṭ/koṇṭakkāl mōṭcam koṭukkumē! koṇṭattūr*
taṇṭaik kāl ammai camaittu vaitta pūcaṇikkāy/aṇṭarkk'ām īcarukkum ām. 195

mere sight of it being capable of sending one to Śiva's world. As a result, the poet concludes, it is more suitable to the celestials, presumably because they are famous for being immortal, as well as for Śiva, who lived despite drinking the Hālahāla poison that rose when the milk ocean was churned. *They* would be safe when consuming this lady's cooking, not mere mortals like himself. In a very similar fashion, in v. 46, he describes his cousin's cooking of a variety of dishes: the description reaches a crescendo in the last line, where he abruptly concludes *uppu kāṇ! cī cī umi!* – 'It is [all] salt! Yuck! Yuck! Spit it!' Introducing this verse as a result of a challenge by a female poet, Puliyūr (2010: 32) claims that the poet embarrassed her with these words.

On another occasion, when Kāḷamēkam assumably perceives how runny buttermilk is, he proceeds to tease the cowherdess who probably had diluted it with water for more profit, by addressing water directly!

> You bear the name 'cloud' when you join the sky;
> You bear the name 'water' after you reach this vast earth;
>> After reaching the hands of the tender-breasted
>>> cowherdesses who churn,
> You bear the name 'buttermilk'!
> You bear all three names![32]

We notice once again that food captures our poet's attention. The last two verses above are part of his more good-natured humour—good-natured possibly

---

[32]*kār enru pēr paṭaittāy kakanatt' urum-pōtu;/ nīr enru pēr paṭaittāy neṭum taraiyil vantatan pin;*
vār onru menmulaiyār āycciyar kai vantatan pin/ mōr enru pēr paṭaittāy! mup pērum perrāyē! 51

for two reasons: first, nothing much is at stake for him, for we have already seen that he becomes incensed when he believes someone to be causing him trouble deliberately or through carelessness. Second, his language remains polite, perhaps because the object of his mockery might be 'respectable' women, either married ones who cooked with good intention but failed miserably, or women who perform a trade assigned to them by their caste (in the case of the cowherdesses). Kālamēkam's tone becomes less gracious when he composes verses, even humorous ones, on devadasis and prostitutes (unless they particularly make his heart flutter and are dear to him).[33] For he abides by the twofold classification of women, namely, the *kulastrī* who belongs to the domain of home and the whore who belongs outside the home. Perhaps there is also a minor third category of women who had to be present in the public space for whatever 'legitimate' reason (e.g. the vegetable vendor in v. 178), whose presence overlaps the two worlds. But to get back to his mocking the devadasis, here is an example, a relatively inoffensive one compared to what will follow:

> The stout *devadāsī* (*tēvaṭiyāḷ*) from life-giving Tirunākai
> Sang with a ruinous voice, and lo and behold!
>> The washerman who lost his donkey yesterday
>> Has come running with a cord,
>> crying 'I have found it! I have found it!'[34]

[33]See fn 55.

[34]*vāḻtta tirunākai vāk' āṉa tēvaṭiyāḷ/ pāḻtta kural eṭuttup pāṭiṉāḷ—nēṟṟuk
kaḻutai keṭṭa vaṇṇāṉ 'kaṇṭēṉ! kaṇṭēṉ!' eṉru/ paḻutaiy eṭutt' ōṭi vantāṉ
pār.* 172

The term that our poet uses to refer to this particular woman, namely, *tēvaṭiyāḷ* (*tēvu* + *aṭiyāḷ* 'servant of god') could point to a devadasi belonging to the Nagapattinam temple. However, her lack of singing skills (compared here to a donkey's braying) hints at her being untrained in the arts necessary to perform her services at the temple. So, she could be a simple prostitute. The poet reacts to bad singing just as he reacts to bad food. While this verse is not particularly malicious, Kālamēkam does seek to produce humour by laughing at another person. Not all verses are this harmless, however, as we come across another devadasi/prostitute being brought down by his scathing words:

The two breasts, which meet [each other], are two bitter-gourds;
The excellent waist is the size of a pestle from the oil-press;
Three parts of the waning hair is entangled
     —for Kalaicci, the wretch,
     whom the dogs from Kamalai-Tiruvārūr desire![35]

While the *kiḷavi* (Puliyūr 2010: 115) explains that the poet was merely retaliating, as Kalaicci (who is said to be a prostitute from Iñcikkuṭi) mocked him, we see him deriding her physical appearance, highlighting the effects of ageing on her body: her breasts, which are shrivelled and sagging like bitter-gourds; her post-menopausal waist that is not as thin as it perhaps was once; and she has a receding hairline—all these only attract lowly dogs in Tiruvārūr, not worthier men like the poet himself. We thus witness Kālamēkam

---

[35]*ēynta taṉaṅkaḷ iraṇṭum iru pākarkāy;/ vāyntav iṭai cekk' ulakkai māttiramē; tēynta kuḻal/ mu-k-kalac cikkum piṭikku(m) mūtēviyāḷ kamalaik/ kukkaḷ iccikkum kalaiccikku.* 183

ridiculing a woman who may have offended him, basing his taunt on her not being in the prime of youth—definitely not to his taste—something that was perhaps deemed essential for her profession. This is one of the many verses in which we observe our poet slighting women (see the section in this chapter titled 'Kāḷamēkam's Values and Worldview'). In general, as mentioned earlier, the devadasis and prostitutes receive a good deal of flak from him, perhaps because he may have felt spite towards them due to their perceived easy virtue, or their boldness, compared to the *kulastrīs*'. But it is also very likely that he had easier access to and better contact with them rather than with the more reclusive wives and mothers of other men, who were deemed the latter's exclusive property. That he looks down upon the prostitutes as a class is evident from v. 215, in which he claims that the priests in Tirukkaṇṇamaṅkai eat nothing but fish from the temple tank and thereby can only be considered the younger brothers of prostitutes (*kūtti*), who represent the destruction of the land. It is evident here that he denigrates the brahmin priests by associating their births with the courtesans', whom he refers to by a pejorative word, namely, *kūtti*.[36] Moreover, he claims that these women bring ruin upon everyone, although this certainly does not seem to deter him from visiting them. This verse also shows that Kāḷamēkam sometimes resorts to women to insult men, as can also be seen from the following verse:

[36]The word, which derives from *kūttu* 'dance', initially meant 'female actor, dancer, dancing girl' (MTL). But the association of temple-dancing with prostitution must have brought about the later meanings of 'courtesan' and 'concubine'.

Why nicely shave the head of Campantāṇṭār
from eternal, sacred Tiruvaṇṇāmalai?
So that the lightning-like slender-waisted women
  do not catch his tuft of hair,
  bend and drag him down,
  and knock on his head![37]

While we could say much about the name Campantāṇṭār, which another poet of some repute apparently shared,[38] this verse ridicules a man for having a shaven head (or even a bald head, perhaps, which the poet wilfully misrepresents?), and also for being beaten up by women, whom he probably teased and/or harassed. In many societies even now, including Tamil society, being slapped or beaten by a woman (other than a motherly figure) is considered far more insulting for a man than being slapped by another man. Thus, the humour that the poet hopes to produce here would not be as effective had

[37]*mannu tiruvaṇṇāmalaic campantāṇṭārkkup/ paṇṇum talaiccavaram paṇṇuvat' ēṉ? —/*
minniṉ ilaittav iṭai mātar ivaṉ kuṭumi paṟṟi/ valaitt' iḻuttuk kuṭṭāmalukku. 47

[38]The life story of the saint-poet Aruṇakirinātar mentions a worshipper of the goddess Kāḷi, a court poet called Campantāṇṭaṉ, who challenged in vain Aruṇakirinātar to make Murukaṉ appear before everyone, just as he would make Kāḷi manifest herself (Venkataramaiah: 1993 [1981]: 332–34). This Campantāṇṭaṉ served Pirapuṭatēva Nāyaṉār, a chieftain who ruled Tiruvaṇṇāmalai and its surroundings, the very town that Kāḷamēkam names as 'his' Campantāṇṭaṉ's hometown. It could have been the same person, although there is no way to confirm this. Please note that the *kiḷavi* of verse 120 (Puliyūr 2010: 79) states that Kāḷamēkam fell ill as a result of calumniating Campantāṇṭaṉ, which might indicate that the latter may have been considered a saint-poet, one of some repute.

Campantāṇṭār been thrashed or snubbed by other men. He thus brings in women to humiliate other men. And this tendency takes on bigger proportions when he apparently insults another man by proxy, by jeering at a woman from his family:

> *āṇṭi kuyavā! aṭā! uṉ peṇṭāṭṭi-taṉai*
> *tōṇṭiy oṉru kēṭṭēṉ. turattiṉāḷ! vēṇṭiy iru*
> *kaikkarakam kēṭṭēṉ, kāl-ataṉait tūkkiyē*
> *cakkarattaik kāṭṭiṉāḷ tāṉ.* 197

> O potter Āṇṭi! Hey!
> I asked your wife for an earthen pot,
>   And she gave me a chase!
> Wishing for palm-sized water pots,
> I asked for two of them!
>   She lifted her leg
>   And showed me her wheel!

First of all, it seems that humour and insult often go hand-in-hand in Kāḷamēkam's mind, especially when dealing with other people. And when a woman is involved, that humour becomes of a sexual nature, just as many swear words used on an everyday basis (across languages) do. In this verse, the poet uses a double-entendre to produce the intended comic effect: *tōṇṭi* is an 'earthen pot' and also a woman's *alkul* ('female genitalia', and sometimes, 'waist').[39] The two 'palm[-sized] water pots' allude to her breasts. But *cakkaram* (<Skt. *cakra-*), literally 'wheel, discus', is more of an enigma: in the context of pottery, it refers to the potter's wheel, and as for the woman's body, the context clearly hints at her genitalia, as Puliyūr (2010:

---

[39]According to Puliyūr (2010: 123), it is likely a metaphor triggered by the shape of a *tōṇṭi*.

123) himself states, albeit with a euphemism (*maṟaiviṭam* 'hidden place'). While none of the dictionaries (Tamil or Sanskrit) that I checked offers any such meaning, it is possible that the poet is alluding to one of the eight *cakra*s, possibly the sacral *cakra*, which would be a euphemism for genitalia here. Thus, it seems that the poet's aim is to offer outrageous insult to another man by casting a slur on his wife's morals. Otherwise, he could very easily have composed a verse solely on the woman with no mention of a man, as is his wont while focusing on devadasis and prostitutes. However, it is likely that these people never existed for real in this specific case: the pottery setting must have offered the poet the possibility of producing a *śleṣa* with these particular words. The lack of a town or village name (which he appears to include in his verses about real people) seems to indicate that we are dealing with a fictional context here, which explains why Kāḷamēkam dares to produce such poetry that can be considered lewd with reference to another man's wife: being another man's property in a patriarchal society, she would be untouchable (in the non-Indian sense of the word).[40] What matters here, however, is how

[40]There might be another exception to this rule, as the poet apparently insults a man for committing incest with his daughter (according to Puliyūr 2010: 118, for example):

Kuṭṭic Cĕṭṭi/The short Cĕṭṭi, who sells goods in Eṭṭikkuḷam,
Took his daughter away and copulated [with her].
And for that, a thousand elephants, seven hundred buffalo bulls
　with humps,
And eighty-five leaping buffalo bulls! 188.

ĕṭṭi kulattiliruntu carakku viṟkum/ kuṭṭicĕṭṭi taṉmakaḷaik koṇṭupōy-
　noṭṭutaṟkē

the poet depicts most women in the name of humour (or otherwise), a topic we shall deal with in the next chapter.[41]

Second, this verse is reminiscent of one of Kaṭuveḷi Cittar's philosophical poems, which involves a Śaiva mendicant who obtains an earthen pot from a potter:

> *nantavaṉattil ōr āṇṭi – avaṉ*
> *nālāṟu mātam-āyk kuyavaṉai vēṇṭi*
> *koṇṭu vantāṉ oru tōṇṭi – mettak*
> *kūttāṭik kūttāṭip pōṭṭ' uṭaittāṇṭi!*

> A mendicant in a grove:
> he begged the potter for ten months
> and brought an earthen pot.
> Dancing round and round,
> he dropped and broke it, O girl!

This song is allegorical: the mendicant is the individual soul; the grove is *saṃsāra*; the earthen pot is the material body for which he waited for ten long months; the

---

āyiram yāṉai yeḻunūṟu kūṉpakaṭu/ pāyum pakaṭēṉpat taintu. 188

There are two issues here. First of all, this verse has been interpreted differently by scholars: Ceṭṭi gave his daughter a dowry of all the animals enumerated above, in order to get her married and made love to, which does seem like a convincing reading (Piḷḷai 2020 [2006]: 121), although the poet's choice of word *noṭṭu* ('copulate') does express utmost spite. Secondly, Tacarataṉ (1994: 16) points out that the *Pulavar Purāṇam* attributes this verse to Vacaikavi Āṇṭāṉ Kavirāyaṉ. Please note that Śrītaraṉ leaves out this verse, probably because it sounded too indecent to him. See Chapter 1, section 'Kālamēkam's poetry'.

[41]Please note that Piḷḷai (2020 [2006]: 143–44) does not offer any such meanings: he rather interprets it as the potter's wife refusing to sell anything to the man who asks her for various types of vessels made of terracotta. And Śrītaraṉ simply leaves this verse out yet again.

potter is God; and the dance is living pleasurably, which ends in the eventual disintegration of the body obtained after such difficulties. While the meanings of this verse and Kāḷamēkam's above are very different (as are the Cittar verses and Kāḷamēkam's in general), this resemblance (same words with *āṇṭi* and *tōṇṭi*; similar context, with the potter being approached, and so forth) may indicate that Kāḷamēkam knew the poems by the Cittars and reacted to them in a way.

Before we proceed, let me recapitulate what humour is to Kāḷamēkam: whether good-natured or not, the butt of his humour is always someone else, including gods, but never himself. I have not come across a single verse in which he makes fun of himself, one of his flaws, or any of the situations that he finds himself in. The closest that we come to that is in a comical bilingual verse in which he laughs at his own situation, when he expresses the linguistic difficulties that he faced when finding himself spending a night with a Telugu-speaking prostitute:

> *'ēmirā vōri'y enpāḷ; 'entuṇṭi vasti' yenpāḷ.*
> *tām irāc connat' ellām talai kaṭai terintat' illai*
> *pōm irāc cūḻum cōlai porum koṇṭait timmi kaiyil*
> *nām irāp paṭṭa pāṭu naman kaiyil pāṭu tānē.* 179

She would say, '*ēmirā vōri!* (Hey, what is it)?';
she would say, '*entuṇṭi vasti?* (Where are you from?)'
>> That's what she said at night, I couldn't make head or tail
>>> of it!
>> What I went through at the hands of Timmi,
>>> her hair like a grove dark as night,
>> Is like the pain one suffers at Yama's hands.

We can easily imagine the poet recounting his night and the trouble that he had—either to communicate with a prostitute from Andhra or to get her to stop talking—as his listeners smiled in mock sympathy.

Another occasion when Kālamekam makes a self-deprecatory comment (except when he deals with a potential patron, as in v. 6) is when he asserts his superiority for an obviously wrong reason:

> O Māl from Kaṇṇapuram!
> You are greater than Śiva.
> I am greater than you.
>   Listen to this one thing:
> in previous days, you took ten births;
> Śiva has had none.
> No one can count *my* births![42]

Births in the Indian context being associated with *saṃsāra* and unending suffering, boasting about one's innumerable births is ironic, a form of dry humour. Thus, in this verse, which in reality asserts Śiva's superiority over Viṣṇu as well as himself, the poet is indeed making a humble (but not too humble) statement about himself while ostensibly boasting. Thus, as a general rule, Kālamēkam is not seen indulging in self-deprecation, either because he thought too highly of himself or because he was just too insecure to laugh at himself. Perhaps it is that sense of insecurity that pushes him to perceive and speak of women the way he does, which we will now turn our attention to.

---

[42] *kaṇṇapura mālē! kaṭavuḷilum nī atikam,/ unnilumē yān atikam onru kēḷ, munnamē*
un pirappō pattām uyar civanukk' onrum illai,/ en pirappu eṇṇat tolaiyātē. 137

Kāḷamēkam's Values and Worldview

> Where indeed women speak little with words, their
> bodies are the most spoken of because they have the
> most to tell.
>
> —Culianu in Law 1995: 1

In this section, we will take a slightly closer look at Kāḷamēkam's values when it comes to women, and what they tell us about his worldview as a man of his times. Although it is not always wise or even right to chrono-centrically apply a set of modern values to judge people who lived in the past, it would be an omission not to draw the reader's attention (if they have not already noticed it) to the fact that Kāḷamēkam indulges in the objectification of women, especially of a sexual nature. Dealing with how women suffer from internalizing this kind of objectification, Barbara L. Fredrickson and Tomi-Ann Roberts (1997: 174–75) speak of the women's 'experience of being treated *as a body* (or collection of body parts) valued predominantly for its use to (or consumption by) others', with sexual objectification occurring 'whenever a woman's body, body parts, or sexual functions are separated out from her person, reduced to the status of mere instruments, or regarded as if they were capable of representing her.' In short, (sexual) objectification occurs when women are identified with their bodies, 'bodies that exist for the use and pleasure of others'.

In light of this understanding, there are a few things that could be stated about Kāḷamēkam's perception and depiction of women. As mentioned earlier, he was a man of his times and perhaps behaved the way in which he was conditioned to. It is beyond the scope of this book to deal with this topic in any detail, but we have already noticed that in his verses, 'women's bodies are looked at, evaluated, and always potentially objectified' (Fredrickson and Roberts 1997: 175), almost systematically. We saw that this is especially the case when he deals with devadasis and prostitutes, whether with a view to produce humour, to retaliate (v. 183 quoted above, in which he derides the changing body of an ageing prostitute), or even to compose a *śleṣa* verse, as for example in the following case, in which he mostly aims at using clever puns that reveal the similarities between the palmyra tree and a prostitute:

> *kaṭṭit taḻuvutalāl, kāl cērav ēṟutalāl,*
> *eṭṭi paṉṉāṭaiy iḻuttalāl - muṭṭap pōy*
> *ācai vāyk kaḷḷai aruntutalāl, ap- paṉaiyum*
> *vēcaiy eṉalāmē viraintu. 57*

Because one embraces them tightly;
Because one climbs them holding the legs together;
Because one reaches out and draws off
    the palmyra fibre/the loose-textured cloth;
Because one butts against them and
    drinks the desirable toddy with the mouth/
    drinks the toddy from her mouth with desire,
one can promptly say that that palm tree is [like] a
    prostitute![43]

There can be no better example to illustrate sexual objectification, in which these nameless, faceless

---

[43]Puliyūr (2010: 38–9) indicates that the poet's humour is apparent as *ap- paṉaiyum* can be split as *appaṉaiyum*, (therefore, 'the father too can be called a prostitute'). But I do not find this interpretation very convincing, as the mention of the father is out of context here.

women as a group are mere commodities to the poet, objects of sexual gratification. He does not bother to separate these persons from their functions.[44] Also, we saw that women other than prostitutes can be the object of his 'sexualized gazing' (Fredrickson and Roberts 1997: 175) as well: other than the hypothetical woman/potter's wife in v. 197, we also came across the unnamed cowherdesses (v. 51) whom he good-naturedly laughed at for selling diluted buttermilk, with the only physical part of their bodies that he briefly describes being not their faces but their breasts ('the tender-breasted cowherdesses who churn'). This emphasis on, even obsession with, women's breasts, not unusual in Indian literature,[45] is also palpable in another verse in which he sexualizes a vegetable vendor, who was probably selling her produce in the street:

> In the great street where Piḷḷaiyār-Gaṇeśa lives,
> who worships at the feet of the pure (Śiva) who rides
> a white bull,
> there is no one to go before the woman
> who sells creeping bindweed leaves for eating
> and tell her [heavy] breasts that her waist will break![46]

[44]Kālamēkam has composed three similar verses comparing prostitutes with a less-than-ideal entity (with a coconut tree in v. 58; with a betel leaf in v. 59; and with a monkey in v. 61).

[45]In canto 7 of the *Naiṣadhīyacarita*, for example, Śrīharṣa describes how Nala's gaze compulsively came back and reposed on Damayantī's breasts.

[46]*vellaiy āṉ ēṟum vimalar aṭi paṇiyum/ piḷḷaiyār vāḻum perum teruvil*
– vallai
ilaik kaṟi viṟpāḷ maruṅkul iṟṟu viṭum eṉṟu/ mulaikk' aṟivippār ilaiyē
muṉ. 178

Once again, the eroticized breasts and waist become the whole person for the poet, as for many others before him, as his gaze wanders with interest over the body of an unknown woman, who may or may not have enjoyed being stripped naked by his eyes. Here is another example:

> *intō tilaka nutal? rāma rāmā! vaṉaca*
> *kontō kaḷapa mulai? kōvintā! – cantam uṟum*
> *vēlō iṉai viḷikaḷ? vēṅkaṭavā! nalla vayi-*
> *r' āl ō kāṇ nārāyaṇā!* 25

> Is her forehead with a *tilaka* the moon? Rāma! Rāma!
> Are her perfumed breasts a cluster of lotuses? Govinda!
> Are her two eyes beautiful lances? Lord of Veṅkaṭam!
> Nice belly, Oh, look, Nārāyaṇa!

Other than being irreverent in this verse, entirely made up of clichéd metaphors, rhetorical questions, and vocatives—for he uses God's names to express his excitement at perceiving an attractive woman[47]—the poet allows his 'sexualized gaze' to spread all over her body. Once again, she does not have an identity here, and so, it could be a woman that he did not know but simply caught sight of somewhere. Even when cursing a woman in anger, as we saw in v. 174, a protective mother who supposedly wished him dead, he replies with, 'Oh lady with mountain[-like breasts akin to] the tusks of a wild elephant with thick musth!' For all we know, it may have been his leering that earned him her rebuke in the first place.

And when he needs to berate a woman in a spiteful way, especially a prostitute, it is their physical

---

[47]In an Abrahamic context, he would have been considered as taking God's name in vain.

appearance, especially the signs of ageing, that he attacks in order to shame them. In v. 183 quoted above, Kāḷamēkam mocks the woman's lack of firm breasts and thin waist—which stand for youth, beauty, and fecundity in a woman—without which the woman is, for him, worthy of contempt. How could such a worthless woman dare stand up to him? We have another example here that will rather fit into the category of poems of abuse (*vacai*):

intu muṭikkum caṭaiyāḷar irukkum toṇṭai vaḷa nāṭṭil,
cintu paṭikkak kavi paṭikkat teriyā maṭavāy! uṉ taṉukkuk-
kentap poṭiy ēṉ? pū-muṭiy ēṉ? kiḻam-āy naraittu mukam tiraintum
inta muṟukk' ēṉ? vīṟāpp' ēṉ? keṭuppēṉ uṉṉaik keṭuppēṉē. 180

In the fertile Toṇṭai land of moon-adorned Śiva with
    matted locks,
Oh ignorant woman who cannot chant *cintu* compositions
    or read poetry!
  Why do you need fragrant powder?
  Why do you need flower adornments?
  Why this impertinence despite your hair greying with age
    and your face now wrinkled?
  Why this arrogance? I shall destroy you, destroy you!

In this verse, Kāḷamēkam is addressing a devadasi, who is traditionally associated with arts and *maquillage* (and perhaps also with perceived pride, which could simply be confidence and self-respect). The poet derides her for not being very artistically accomplished, and wonders why such a woman, who also happens to have become old (hence physically unattractive), could want cosmetics and also express pride physically, and perhaps even challenge him, a man, and a great poet at that! Through his rhetorical questions ('Why this impertinence despite your hair greying with age and your face becoming wrinkled? Why [this] arrogance?'), the poet clearly indicates that pride in a youthful woman might be acceptable, but not in an older woman, who ought to know better and be more self-effacing. The words in this verse are self-explanatory, so suffice it to note the aggressive nature of his last comment, a threat to ruin her. The choice of word could be pertinent, depending on what the poet means by *keṭuppēṉ*: he is threatening to destroy her (*keṭuppēṉ*), but the verb *keṭu* means by extension violating a woman, at least in modern parlance. While the first attestation of this meaning may have occurred later, we cannot entirely rule out the sexual nature of the threat, although, given his professed disgust for older women, he could simply be threatening to ruin her by heaping abuse.[48]

On the whole, we do see that the poet is obsessed with the woman's body parts or with her body as a

[48]The way the prostitutes come across in Kālamēkam's poetry and world can be very different from how they appear in other poets' corpus. For example, it is in stark contrast to how Kṣetrayya from the Telugu land presents them, as Ramanujan, Rao, and Shulman (1994: 18) point out: '. . . the courtesan appears as the major figure in this poetry of love (. . .) She is bold, unattached, free from the constraints of home and family. In some sense, she represents the possibility of choice and spontaneous affection, in opposition to the largely predetermined, and rather calculated, marital tie. She can also manipulate her customers to no small extent (. . .). But above all, the courtesan signals a particular kind of knowledge, one that achieved preeminence in the late medieval cultural order in South India.'

Perhaps Kālamēkam did not befriend the same kind of devadasis, or perhaps he did, and precisely did not like their self-reliance and confidence. The exploration of this fascinating topic is unfortunately beyond the scope of this book.

whole. And more often than not, by focusing on the female body and its sexual functions, he often (but not always[49]) fails to see the person behind that body, which perhaps explains his slighting remarks. This intense obsession with the female body accompanied by a marked contempt for the person seems to be one side of the patriarchal coin, the other being total repulsion felt for both, something that is expressed by poets across time and space, in the Indian subcontinent and beyond. Whether it is the Sanskrit poet Bhartṛhari in his *Vairāgyaśatakam* or the Tamil Cittar poets (the main ones living between the tenth and fifteenth centuries), whose particularly pungent choice of words and misogynistic ideas are startling, the body of the female rarely fails to foster some kind of reaction. Whether it is Pāmpāṭṭi Cittar who denigrates the female body and warns men off in the following way . . .

Dance, Oh snake,
understanding that
    those who, considering the skin that shrinks much as round
        breasts,
    delightedly call them hills of happiness and
    those who have fallen into the well that is the stinking vagina
will be ruined![50]

or Paṭṭiṉattār, who disparages the perceived promiscuity of women thus:

    A hole planted in so many times;
    breasts touched by so many people;

[49]See the end of this chapter.

[50]*vaṭṭa mulai eṉru mika varrum tōlai/ makamēṭu eṉa uvakai vaittuk kūruvār*
keṭṭa nārram uḷḷa yōṉik kēṇiyil viḻntār/ keṭuvar eṉrē tuṇintu āṭu pāmpē!

This verse is quoted by Ñāṉacēkaraṉ 2009: 16.

lips that were bit and pulled by so many people;
　　it is always fake, hey man!
　　On this resounding earth, leave the silly women,
　　And be saved, hey man!
　　Be saved, be saved![51]

. . . what some of the Cittars say about women and their bodies is 'a veritable litany of contempt' (Spelman 1982: 109). We notice that the Cittars, whose poetry Kālamēkam seems to have been aware of—since they probably lived around his time and/or were popular then, as they are still today—were more critical and explicit than their poetic forebears who composed bhakti verses, from whom they differed considerably. As Tē. Ñānacēkaran (2009: 13) points out, these verses cannot be thought to apply only to prostitutes, but to all women in general. This sort of biting criticism of the female and her body simply did not exist in early Tamil poetry, which, as a matter of fact, celebrated both. Scholars such as Ñānacēkaran (2009: 15) have suggested that the influence of Jain and Buddhist thoughts regarding women's bodies must have filtered into Tamil thought.[52] This is too vast (and even irrelevant) a topic to deal with here. Suffice it to say that Kālamēkam must have known some of the Cittar verses and that his language (explicit and even crude like theirs) and outlook were likely influenced by them

[51]*ettanaiyō naṭṭa kuḷi, ettanai pēr toṭṭa mulai/ ettanai pēr parri iḷutta itaḷ—nittam nittam*
poyyaṭā! pēcum puviyil maṭa mātarai viṭṭu/ uyyaṭā! uyyaṭā! uy!

This verse is quoted by Ñānacēkaran 2009: 12.

[52]Somatophobia (especially of the female body) in Sanskrit (and world) literature has also been discussed by scholars such as Shah 2009.

to an extent: for while he does not hate women or their bodies (and could even be one of the women-loving men described by the Cittars), he does seem to bear in general an inherent repugnance for them, seemingly incompatible with attraction except when it comes to ageing bodies.

Having said this, Kālamēkam uses restraint while speaking of women on certain occasions. Even when poking fun at his hostesses with deplorable cooking skills (see v. 7 in the preceding section), he uses proper language and does not allow his eyes to roam either. For example, in v. 7, he speaks of 'the anklet-footed lady from Koṇṭattūr', almost as if he did not look up above her feet, reminding one of Lakṣmaṇa's words in the *Rāmāyaṇa*, in which he claims not to recognize Sītā's other ornaments, but just her anklets, since he prostrated himself before her feet every day (4.6.22), implying that her feet were her only body parts that he had seen.[53] Our poet also refrains from describing any of the body parts of the women who cooked for him (v. 46 and 192). So Kālamēkam does not exercise 'the socially sanctioned right of all males to sexualise all females, regardless of age or status' (Westkott 1986: 95), as he makes an exception for 'respectable' women who belong to other men and whom he encounters at home.[54] Perhaps he believes them to belong to the

---

[53]This verse is not part of the critical edition.

[54]We have already seen how leering he can become when spotting women in the street, married or otherwise, when they find themselves outside the protection granted by home—as defined by patriarchy. But Kālamēkam finds a way to speak of the breasts of 'respectable' women who stay inside home as well, under the acceptable pretext of congratulating a man on the birth of a son:

roles that patriarchal society has assigned to them (e.g. housewives should be at home and cook, prostitutes should be good-looking and willing to please). Or he could be showing respect to women who feed him. Or perhaps they were women from his own family, as he refers to an aunt's daughter (*attai makaḷ*) in one of the three verses mentioned above (v. 46) and also calls one of them *āccāḷ* (v. 196), which is either a proper noun or else a word meaning 'mother'. Therefore, the poet could be referring either to his own parent, or another woman whom he respectfully addresses thus, as is the custom of the land. Is respect for women then reserved for women of his own family, if at all they were related to him?

We must admit at this point that there are a few other women whom our poet does praise in an entirely

---

kañca mukaiyum kaḷirrāṉaiyiṉ kompum/ añcu(m) mulai nālu(m) mulaiy āṉatuvum, miñcu pukaḷ
perrāṉ-taṉ mālai piṟark' aḷittatum kutalai/ karrāṉ piṟanta-piṉpu kāṇ. 171

The breasts that were feared by the lotus buds and the tusks of
   male elephants
turning into drooping breasts [and]
Perrāṉ of superior fame offering his desire to others
Happened after the lisping [baby] was born, see! 171.

Kālamēkam celebrates the arrival of a baby by indicating the physical changes in its mother, who has become less sexually attractive after childbirth, reminding us of the words *prasavānte ca yauvanam* 'Youth [in a woman] ends with the delivery [of a child]', which are probably from a floating verse but are quoted by Śrīvaiṣṇava Ācāryas (Anandakichenin 2024: 169 fn 717). Please note that Puliyūr (2010: 109–10) interprets the husband's changes in his affections as being directed towards other women as a result, reflecting the changes in his wife's body and perhaps in her wants, which the poet allows himself to comment upon.

non-sexual way—and they are no *kulastrī*, but rather devadasis and prostitutes that he is fond of. Let us check out this example:

Seeing the beauty of Cōmi from Ārrūr of the refined, threefold Tamil,
Nārāyaṇa grew really faint (*neṭumāl*);
then, the four-faced [Brahmā] rode a thousand *maṭal*;
the heavenly Kāma lost his form;
And the famous king of heaven (Indra) obtained a thousand eyes![55]

Kāḷamēkam hyperbolically praises Cōmi's beauty to the skies, speaking of its mesmerizing influence that made all gods enamoured (except for the destroyer of Kāma, Śiva!): he rewrites mythology for them, so to speak, or gives a different explanation to their names. Thus, Kāma loses his form not because Śiva burnt him to ashes, but because Cōmi's beauty annihilated him; and Nārāyaṇa grew faint rather than cause confusion (*māl*), the latter being the accepted etymological meaning of this Tamil name; Brahmā rides a *maṭal* like a desperate man in love; and finally, Indra did not get a thousand eyes/vaginas as a punishment for seducing Ahalyā but rather to admire Cōmi's beauty better.[56] The poet abstains from describing Cōmi's different body parts or focusing on her breasts, for example, as he has done with other women, whatever their background. Similarly, while describing another

---

[55]*ārāyum muttamil ārrūril cōmi aḷaku kaṇṭu/ nārāyaṇan neṭu māl ākiṉāṉ; marrai nāṉmukaṉum/ ōr āyiram maṭal ūrntāṉ; viṇ māraṉ uru aḷintāṉ/ pērāṉa vāṉavar kōṉum kaṇ āyiram perraṉaṉē!* 182

[56]This verse, suspected to have been misattributed to Kāḷamēkam, may have been composed by Āṇṭāṉ since he too has sung about Cōmi from Ārrūr (Tacaratan 1994: 49–50).

family of devadasis,[57] Kāḷamēkam shows his tender side:

> The eyes of Kūttāḷ are long, sharp spears;
> The eyes of Kūttāḷ's elder sister are fully dark blue;
> The eyes of the mother of the elder sister are lotuses;
> The eyes of the mother's mother are two arrows![58]

This is probably the simplest verse that Kāḷamēkam wrote: no real alliterations, no puns, no extravagant words or ideas, but a little bit of humour, as he was perhaps indulging the request of this family to praise them. And although these are clearly women whom Kāḷamēkam approached for sexual favours or some such entertainment, he does not give a graphic description of their body parts or their lovemaking, but solely focuses on their eyes.[59] Thus, we do notice that our poet can abstain from sexualizing even a prostitute's body if he is fond enough of her, probably a response to her own affectionate attitude towards him, which takes the edge off his temper and tongue. When Kāḷamēkam manages to see the person behind

[57]The name Kūttāḷ 'she who dances' shows that this is a family of devadasis, not just prostitutes.

[58]*kūttāḷ viḷikaḷ neṭum kūr vēlām; kūttāḷ-tan̠/ mūttāḷ viḷikaḷ muḻu nīlam – mūttāḷ-tan̠*

āttāḷ viḷikaḷ aravintam; āttāḷ-tan̠/ āttāḷ viḷikaḷ iraṇṭ' ampu. 173

[59]Attributing this verse to Poyyāmoḻi Pulavar, an anonymous blogger, offers a different context to this verse, by stating that the above poet sings this verse in praise of visually-challenged women, with whom he later trusts money only to be betrayed. For more on this, see the blog post at http://tamilagam52. blogspot.com/2020/07/blog-post.html. We thus notice that the Tamil poets have indeed inspired many stories such as this that have lasted the test of time.

the woman's body, he does not dehumanize or objectify her. Although there are very few poems to show us this other, gentler side, it is worth noting its presence.

CHAPTER THREE

Kāḷamēkam, the Poet, the Devotee

WHILE KĀḶAMĒKAM HAS composed verses on various topics, he mentions/praises one or many deities/temple(s) in approximately 130 verses (out of over 216 verses attributed to him[1]), which consists of a whopping 60 per cent of his poetry, roughly speaking. Thus, gods always seem to be present at the back of his mind, their temples being part of his everyday life, providing him with a pool of ideas from which he can pick topics, stories, and images. It does seem that our poet knew the Āḻvārs' and Nāyaṉmārs' poetry as well.[2] In that case, we may wonder if Kāḷamēkam followed in their footsteps, or if he innovated and

[1]Both numbers are based on Puliyūr's (2010) edition, provided here to give an idea of the number of temples and deities that were at the back of the poet's mind.

[2]That Kāḷamēkam knew their poetry can be seen through various ways: for example, he is thought to allude to Tirumaḻicai Āḻvār in v. 170 as he mentions *karrāṉ piṉ ceṉra karuṇai māl* 'the compassionate Māl who followed the cows with calves (*karru* + *āṉ*)/ the learned person (*karrāṉ*)', i.e. Tirumaḻicai Āḻvār. To know more about this story, see Anandakichenin 2022. Also, in v. 136, Kāḷamēkam writes a verse that is reminiscent of Periyāḻvār's verse *attattiṉ pattām nāḷ* 'tenth day from the Attam/Hastam [asterism]' in which he plays with the names of asterisms while giving Kṛṣṇa's birth details (*Periyāḻvār Tirumoḻi* 1.2.6). We can cite many such examples.

forged his own path. Did he express emotions similar to the ones he felt toward fellow humans, or did he show more reverence toward the divine? But most of all, one wonders, in light of the kind of verses we have read so far, whether his god-related verses can be called bhakti poetry, and him a bhakti poet.

Before we focus on Kāḷamēkam's 'bhakti' verses, we need to remember that certain features characterize first-millennium Tamil bhakti poetry, as pointed out by Friedhelm Hardy in his seminal work *Viraha Bhakti* (first published in 1983): a personal kind of devotion, which allows the saint-poet to feel close to God, who is present locally in a shrine/temple (which is also celebrated), in a tangible form (often described elaborately), whom they address in their mother tongue, sometimes in a familiar (even a mock-insulting) way. Perhaps as a result of all this, their devotion is (often) of an emotional kind, with the poet pining for the Lord, desperate for union, feeling possessed, and so forth. And sometimes, loyalty to their deity of choice could push a saint-poet to belittle the others, both the 'opponent others' and the 'wholly others', to borrow Hirst's expressions (2008), effectively used by Gil Ben-Herut (2018), precisely while dealing with Śaiva bhakti poets in Kannada. How much of all this do we find in Kāḷamēkam's poetry? Can pride, humour, sarcasm, and so forth be found in these 'bhakti verses' as well?

Devotional Verses

> Bhakti is here an overpowering, even suffocating emotion, which causes tears to flow and the voice to

> falter, and even stimulates hysterical laughter, loss of
> consciousness, and trance.
>
> —Gonda 1948: 640; tr. Hardy 1983: 38

Friedhelm Hardy (1983: 38) reacts to the above words of Gonda's concerning the *Bhāgavata Purāṇa* and establishes throughout his pathbreaking book that the Āḻvārs' (and Nāyaṉmārs') bhakti poetry, which was strongly influenced by classical Tamil poetry, is one of the inspirations for the emotions found in this Purāṇa. Whether Āḻvār poetry influenced the Purāṇa or they both had a common source, we need to remember that one of the chief characteristics of this kind of poetry is all-encompassing emotion. Let us now see if Kāḷamēkam, who was clearly knowledgeable about the Itihāsas and the Purāṇas as most of his contemporary Tamil poets worth the name would be, followed in the footsteps of his predecessors.

Our poet did not mean his self-contained verses to be part of one homogeneous poetic work, so there are no invocatory verses per se. However, modern editors of his corpus, like Puliyūr (2010) and Śrītaraṉ (2013), have chosen to begin their editions with verses that could be used as invocations, perhaps following in the footsteps of the manuscripts. If we begin with those two verses, dedicated to Gaṇeśa and Sarasvatī, respectively, we might be able to understand what a standard 'bhakti verse' looks like when it comes from Kāḷamēkam:

> If one worships the warrior elephant-calf
>> that [Śiva] gave to my elephant [goddess] who dwells in
>>> delightful Āṉaikkā,
> There will be knowledge that is not obtained [elsewhere];
> there will be bhakti;

there will be birth of children;
there will be power,
and there will be success.[3]

We see that this verse in *veṇpā* metre boasts of proper *etukai* (second syllable) rhymes; an alliteration in [*t*] in the second half of the verse, and a pun on the word *āṉai*.[4] It includes mention of a specific temple (Āṉaikkā), although there are no descriptions of it, stereotyped or otherwise, except perhaps for a hint at the Sthalapurāṇa/*talapurāṇam*[5] (which includes an elephant worshipping Śiva), perhaps veiled by a Purāṇic event (Śiva and Devī begetting Gaṇeśa).[6] The verse also lists all the good things that one will obtain by worshipping this god at this specific place (most of them some kind of material benefit), which makes it sound like a *phalaśruti* verse (which enunciates the fruits of reciting a sacred work), except that the fruit is *not* generated by the recitation of the verse, but rather by the worship of the deity. However, the poet does not express his devotion or humility, nor does he really praise the god or ask for his support or

---

[3]*ēr āṉaikkāvil uṟaiy eṉṉ āṉaikk' aṉr' aḷitta/ pōr āṉaik kaṉṟu-taṉaip pōṟṟiṉāl—vārāta putti varum patti varum puttirav uṟpatti varum/ catti varum citti varum tāṉ.* 1

[4]Since Gaṇeśa is an elephant, the poet seems to call his mother a female elephant here, with whom Śiva begot Gaṇeśa. It is also worth remembering that the Sthalapurāṇa of the temple involves an elephant, which also explains the name of the temple-town (*āṉai+kā* 'elephant forest').

[5]For more on Sthalapurāṇas/*talapurāṇams*, see Shulman 1980: 29–39.

[6]According to one version of the story, Śiva and Devī turned into elephants and produced Gaṇeśa.

protection. No expression of love or longing can be discerned, nor any betrayal of emotion (if at all he felt any). Can this be called a bhakti verse? It seems to me that it can only because it deals with one of the many gods that he seems to have worshipped. With a few exceptions, this is roughly how Kālamēkam composes bhakti poetry, which tends to be very different from the Āḻvārs' and Nāyanmārs' corpus, although not all poems belonging to the latter possess the features mentioned above.

The verse presented as the second invocation by Puliyūr (2010: 2) is dedicated to Sarasvatī:

> Wearing white clothes,
> adorning herself with white jewellery,
> she would sit upon a white lotus—
> the mother
> who seated me as an equal
> alongside kings on white thrones.[7]

This is a much simpler verse, neither clever in terms of ideas, nor breathtaking in terms of sounds and rhyme, with the *etukai* in the first two lines depending upon the same word with the same meaning, namely, *veḷḷai* ('white'), repeated four times in the verse. But, although it is not uncommon to speak of the goddess in this way, it draws the listener's attention to the goddess's white purity, a feature that identifies her as Sarasvatī even when she is not named. And although the poet once again does not express any praise nor ask for protection, and although he does not explicitly

---

[7] *veḷḷaik kalaiy uṭuttu, veḷḷaip paṇi pūṇṭu/ veḷḷaik kamalattil vīrr' iruppāḷ*
— *veḷḷai*
ariyācaṉattil aracarōṭ' eṉṉaic/ cariy ācaṉam vaitta tāy. 2

convey gratitude nor betray any emotions, all these can be palpable if we look carefully: being the goddess of learning, she took the poet under her wing and placed him on par with kings—one of the highest honours of his day and time—clearly by bestowing knowledge and poetic skills upon him. She thus becomes a mother figure to him, and it is perhaps by using that term that the poet betrays his gratitude as well as some emotion.

On the whole, these two verses seem rather formal, which is perhaps why some modern editors (and perhaps their palm-leaf-and-stylus-using forebears collecting verses and writing them down in one place) opted for presenting them as invocations. Do all his other 'bhakti' verses resemble these two? It is worth remembering that Kāḷamēkam sometimes uses gods as his topics, especially when experimenting with poetry or to show his poetic prowess. We have already discovered some of his *śleṣa* verses that put on par a deity and a worldly, insentient entity, e.g. Viṣṇu and a betel leaf (see Chapter 1, v. 67). Let us now look at another verse, seemingly composed to fulfil the condition of mentioning the names of the trinity (Śiva, Viṣṇu, and Brahmā, in that order) and listing their food, weapon, ornaments, vehicles, and dwelling places, and all this in the *veṇpā* metre (Puliyūr 2010: 26). Kāḷamēkam proceeds to deal with these deities in an interesting way:

For the Vedic [Brahmā], Hara, and Māl-Nārāyaṇa,
    boy, butter, pulses are [their *kaṟi* 'vegetables/poison'];
    superior paddy, poison, earth [are their food];
    deer, discus, staff [are their weapons];
    sapphire, [sacred] thread, spotted snake [are their ornaments];

white bull, bird (Garuḍa), *haṃsa* [are their vehicles];
rock, deep [sea], lotus [are their abodes].[8]

While trying to fit all this information pertaining to three gods in a metrical composition, Kāḷamēkam gives it in a random order, based on what is said of the deities in texts such as the Purāṇas. Here is a table that will give a clearer idea of the contents of the verse:

TABLE 2: Contents of Verse 36[9]

	Brahmā	*Hara-Śiva*	*Māl-Nārāyaṇa*
Vegetables/ meat	pulses	boy	butter
food	superior paddy	poison	earth
weapon	staff	deer	discus
ornament	sacred thread	spotted snake	sapphire
vehicle	*haṃsa*	white bull	bird [Garuḍa]
abode	lotus	Rock[y mountain]	deep [sea]

[8]*ciṟuvaṉ, aḷai, payaṟu; cem nel, kaṭuku, pū;/ maṟi, tikiri, taṇṭu; maṇi nūl − poṟi aravam*

veḷēṟu, puḷ, aṉṉam; vētaṉ araṉ mālukku/ kal, tāḻam, pūvē, kari. 36

[9]Please note that Brahmā is said to eat pulses and paddy; he holds a staff and is invested with a sacred thread; he rides the goose-like *haṃsa* bird and lives upon a lotus that sprouted from Nārāyaṇa's navel. Śiva requested human flesh for consumption in Ciṟutoṇṭar's life-story, and eats the Hālahāla poison that emerges from the churned milk ocean in order to protect the world; he holds a deer, wears a snake, rides upon Nandi, a bull, and lives on the Kailāsa peak in the Himalayas. Nārāyaṇa eats butter as Kṛṣṇa, and swallows the whole world during dissolution; he holds the discus-weapon, wears sapphire, rides a kite, and reclines on the milk ocean.

While this verse bears witness to Kāḷamēkam's poetic accomplishment, it definitely cannot be called a bhakti verse, for no devotion is expressed, hinted at, or even intended here. Any other objects or commonly-known people could have easily replaced the trinity. This is not the kind of content that we come across in the Āḻvārs' or the Nāyanmārs' poetry. The same goes for the following verse by our poet:

Oh lord of Veṅkaṭam of admirable glory!
Come, be born in half a *venpā* according to my desire!
> O fish! O tortoise! O boar! O lion! O dwarf! O [Paraśu]
> Rāma! O Rāma!
> O [Bala]Rāma! O cowherd! O you who will be a horse
> [Kalkin]![10]

This popular verse, which manages to enumerate Viṣṇu-Nārāyaṇa's ten avatāras, is once again more of a list than a devotional verse, with only a prayer (or rather, an order!) to Viṣṇu telling him that he should appear in the poet's half-verse in all ten forms. Once again, Kāḷamēkam seems more interested in showing his poetic prowess than in expressing devotion, in fitting lists into his chosen metres. These verses are indeed a far cry from what we find in Tamil bhakti poetry: there is no pining, no crying, no being possessed, no pleading. Does that mean that Kāḷamēkam did not feel anything for God, other than perhaps anger (as we shall see later)?

Not quite. Let us have a look at the following verse:

Oh handsome lord wearing a saree!
Oh undivided lord of the gods!

---

[10]*meccu pukaḻ vēṅkaṭavā! venpāvil pātiyil eṉ/ iccaiyil uṉ ceṉmam etukkavā – maccā! kūr-
mā! kōlā! ciṅkā! vāmā! rāmā! rāmā! rā-/ mā! kōpālā! mā āvāy!* 28

Oh handsome lord with garlands of purple waterlilies!
Oh lord with a beautiful chest!
Oh lord of Ārūr who burned down the city of people unruly
    like the sea!
Oh Vītiviṭaṅka!
    Your bull is inseparable from you.[11]

This verse, dedicated to Śiva enshrined in Tiruvārūr, consists of a set of vocatives addressed to that deity (including his processional form, Vītiviṭaṅkan). The poet uses positive vocabulary highlighting both the lord's physical beauty, upon which he lingers, as well as his lordliness and exploits. Thus he shows his admiration, fondness, and even a certain joy, although the poem does not contain any expression of salutation or request per se. The poet's conclusive words might even hint at his wish to serve as Śiva's inseparable bull, which would allow him to admire all these qualities of the lord from very close quarters. This verse is very much reminiscent of the bhakti poets' style and contents. The following verse, too, shows Kāḷamēkam's pleasure in being engrossed in the divine couple's union:

āṟāt' orukkālu maiyām ēkamparukku
māṟā vaṭuvāy maṟaiyātē-pēṟākac
ceṅkaiyiṉālēy aluttic ceyya kaccik kāmāṭci
koṅkaiyiṉāl iṭṭa kuṟi. 155

The marks
    —made by the breasts of perfect Kāmākṣī from
        Kanchipuram,
    who pressed against him with her fair arms,

[11]*cēlaiy uṭaiy aḻakā! tēvar akaṇṭā! kaḻunīr/ mālaiy aḻakā! maṇimārpā!*
vēlai
aṭaṅkār puram erittav ārurā! vīti/ viṭaṅkā! piriyā viṭai. 210

considering that her good fortune—
will not fade,
never healing,
becoming ink[-like],
and turning into eternal scars for Ekampar.

This verse could have come straight out of Kālidāsa's *Kumārasambhavam*, as Kālamēkam tastefully points out that this godly warrior is proudly wearing the love-battle scars made by his beloved on his chest. While the beauty of her breasts stands for her beauty as a whole, our poet also points out her devotion toward Śiva, both as a god and a husband; she considers embracing him her privilege, not his. And since her love is eternal, so are the marks that she made. When reading through his poetry, we find that Kālamēkam has a soft spot for Devī, perhaps even more so than for Śiva himself. A certain tenderness creeps into his tone when he sings about her. But when all is said and done, we still have not read any verse that could sound more like a bhakti verse with petitions and requests for protection or liberation, for a vision of the lord, a declaration of the inability to protect oneself, or a professing of one's own inferiority. However, after going through his whole corpus of *taṇippāṭal*s, I came upon the following verse:

> *nīr' āvāy neṟṟi, nerupp' āvāy aṅkam, iru*
> *kūr' āvāy mēṇi, koḷuttuvāy – māṟāta*
> *naṭṭam ūvāy, cōṟu nañc' āvāy. nāyēṇai*
> *iṭṭam-āy kāppāy iṇi.* 14

> You have holy ash on the forehead;
> you have a body made of fire;
> your body has two parts;
> you blaze away;

> you dance unceasingly;
> you have poison for food.
> *Now protect the dog who is me!* (emphasis mine)

Note the expression of self-deprecation in the last line ('the dog, who is me') along with an entreaty ('Now willingly protect me'). And this humble request is very much in contrast to Kālamēkam's spirit: it usually sounds as if he would more likely have forced Śiva into protecting him. This kind of sentiment is rather rare in Kālamēkam's poetry and figures here as an exception that proves the rule.

Still, few are the verses through which our poet pours out strong emotions. Speaking of Cuntarar, David Shulman (1990: xxiv) recognizes 'an expansion on the level of identity, and a sense of being taken over, driven, moved by forces beyond one's control. The deity enters into the poet, pervades his being, fills him from within—and bursts out of him in song.' This could more or less apply to many of the Tamil bhakti poets, but not to Kālamēkam. There is no erotic feeling either when talking about the gods, and it seems to me that the only vehement emotion that our poet feels is anger, when he is not overcome with a sense of the ridicule. Let us now focus on Kālamēkam's wicked side that he shows to the gods as well, which partly—only partly—echoes the bhakti poets.

The *Nindā-stuti*

Kālamēkam can present a perfectly proper topic in ways that may appear innocuous, but that show a certain irreverence on his part. In the following verse, for instance, he describes the effects of Yaśodā's smacking of Kṛṣṇa on the universe:

The eight elephants [of the direction],
the great Mount Meru,
the oceans,
the earth,
and everything else moved,
>   when flies swarmed around the wound
>   caused by blows of a big churning staff
>   of the cowherdess (Yaśodā) whose words are music.[12]

When Kṛṣṇa moved (perhaps due to the sensation of tickling producing by flies buzzing around an unhealed wound), the rest of the world, which depends on him (or which is inside him, as the *Mañcari* suggests, p. 248), swayed along. And while this verse indicates the divine nature of Kṛṣṇa and is even reminiscent of many humorous Sanskrit *muktaka* ('floating') verses—including the one that states that Nārāyaṇa chose to inhabit the middle of the milk ocean in order to escape bed bug bites[13]— it does betray a certain irreverence towards the god. Speaking lightly of a festering wound on Kṛṣṇa's body that attracts flies is not very reverential, to say the least. It is definitely unlike the Āḻvārs' thoughts or words, for example. Periyāḻvār, for example, worries that Kṛṣṇa's black body might get tired if he goes grazing cows in the

[12]*vāraṇaṅkaḻeṭṭu(m), makamēruvum, kaṭalum,/ tāraṇiyum ellāñ calittaṉav āl! − nāraṇaṉaip*
paṇ-vāy iṭaicci paru mattiṉāl aṭitta/ puṇ-vāyil īmoytta pōtu.

Please note that Puliyūr's (2010) edition does not include this verse but both Piḷḷai's (v. 38) and Śrītaraṉ's (v. 154) do.

[13]*kamale kamalā śete haraś śete himālaye| kṣīrābadhau ca hariḥ śete manye matkuṇaśaṅkayā ||*

'I believe that Kamalā lies in the lotus; Hara-Śiva, in the Himalayas; and Hari-Viṣṇu, in the milk ocean, out of fear of [bed] bugs'.

forest (*Periyālvār Tirumoli* 2.7.1), while Kulacēkara Ālvār feels inconsolable at the thought of Rāma's 'soft feet exuding blood as the stones pierce them like the tips of spears in the hands of enemies' (*Perumāl Tirumoli* 9.5). In the case of Kālamēkam, however, he seems to enjoy his own imagination, and the verse that he produces as a result. As we saw earlier on, this poet is not very prone to getting emotional while speaking of/to the gods in his verses (except on occasion), and certainly does not seem to feel sorry for them. Also irreverent is his tone when wondering whether Śiva consumed poison to commit suicide, a topic that he broaches in v. 119, as he does in a handful of other verses:

Were you ashamed of being pelted with stones (by the Jains)?
Or of being kicked by (Kaṇṇappaṉ's) foot?
Or of being lashed by (Arjuna's) bow?
    Oh [lord] of Āṉaikkā with tall walls that adorn
      themselves with clouds!
    Why did you eat poison that day?[14]

Once again, nothing insulting per se: if anything, the poet is trying to understand Śiva's act as one would a fellow human's, by comparing his drinking the Hālahāla poison to save the world as an act of attempted suicide motivated by a sense of humiliation. We are already venturing into the territory of *nindā-stuti*, since Kālamēkam is in a way ridiculing Śiva by presenting him as a victim. Please note that elsewhere

---

[14]*kallāl aṭittataṟkō, kālāl utaittataṟkō,/ villāl aṭittataṟkō, veṭkiṉīr? colvīr, āl!*
mañcu-taṉai cūṭum uyar matil āṉaikkāvārē!/ nañcu-taṉait tiṉṟat' eṉ munnāl? 161

he likens his drinking poison to saving the world, so if he had intended insult here, it is only superficial. In v. 96, he lists many of the occasions when Śiva was hit with something, only to wonder whether it was the absence of parents that caused him to be treated so badly by everyone (*ampalavāṇarkk' ōr aṉṉai pitā illāta tāḻvō?* 'Was the insult [caused] by Ampalavāṇaṉ-Śiva's lack of a mother and a father?'). And yet, he lauds Śiva for being birthless, which explains why he does not have parents in the first place, in another verse (v. 137, quoted above). Similarly, when he apparently shows pity on him in the following way . . .

> O lord of Puliyūr in the South! If you are simple,
>> Won't a woman jump up and climb upon your head?
>> Won't a man hit you with a worn sandal?
>> Won't another man insult you and break his bow on your body?[15]

. . . there is no real, direct blame, *nindā*, though there is no reverence for a god that he judges to be the highest.

[15]*tāṇṭiy orutti talaiyiṉ-mēl ēṟālō?/ pūṇṭa ceruppāl oruvaṉ pōṭāṉō —
mīṇṭ' oruvaṉ
vaiyāṉō vil muṟiya māṭṭāṉō teṉpuliyūr/ aiyā nīy ēḻai yāṉāl.* 92

'Won't a woman jump up and climb upon your head?' is a reference to the river Ganges that flowed from heaven onto Śiva's matted locks, before he let it flow down to the earth. This story is narrated in the 'Bālakāṇḍa' of Vālmīki's *Rāmāyaṇa*. 'Won't a man hit you with a worn sandal?' is a reference to Śiva's hunter-devotee Kaṇṇappa Nāyaṉār, who placed his foot on the eye of Śiva's image in order to know its exact location. To know the full story, see Cēkkiḻār's *Periya Purāṇam* 1.16. 'Won't another man Insult you and break his bow [beating you up]' is an allusion to an event in the *Mahābhārata* ('Vana parvan'), in which Arjuna fights with Śiva, who appears disguised as a hunter.

Modern editors (e.g. Puliyūr 2010: 60) tend to tag this as a *nindā-stuti*, but it is more subtle than the direct *nindā-stuti* that we shall examine now.

For Kālamēkam can go much further than using a casual, irreverent tone; he can speak to and of the gods as he does of fellow humans, as an equal. This is mostly visible in his *nindā-stuti*s (*vacaippāṭal* in Tamil), which comprise a large part of his 'bhakti' verses. Insulting gods in order to laud them is nothing new in Indian literature. Even the Āḻvārs and the Nāyaṉmārs have done that, especially in the case of Śiva for his looks, practices, and idiosyncrasies. However, as Nancy Ann Nayar (1992: 74fn25) asserts, 'The idea behind *nindā-stuti* is that God is so great that even censure cannot hurt Him; consequently, to speak words of censure is to proclaim His greatness'. This is how Śiva's drawbacks are celebrated—albeit disguised as blame—by many poets across time. And for Kālamēkam, who thrives on sarcasm and mockery, this is unsurprisingly a favourite genre.

Let us begin by looking at an example of a bhakti poem that incorporates *nindā*: the following is by the Śaiva saint Cuntarar, 'the harsh devotee', referring to whom Shulman (1990: xxvi) rightly speaks of 'confrontational consciousness—his peculiar combination of angry rejection, unscrupulous blackmail, chutzpah, and intimate connection':

> At all times,
> whether they are rewarded
> Or not,
> your servants worship your anklets
> with love.
> You know they have no other support,

and still you have no compassion,
you act
without wisdom or reason.
And if, lord,
they become wholly destitute and afflicted,
in a moment of disaster,
can they mortgage you for food,
you who are in Ōṇakāntintaḷi? [44][16] (*Tēvāram* 7.5.3;
     tr. Shulman 1990: 31; emphasis mine)

No doubt Cuntarar speaks casually to Śiva as one does to a friend, for which he rightly earned the title of *tampirāṉ tōḻar* ('lord's friend'). However, although he accuses his favourite deity of lacking reason and perhaps of lacking compassion too, and wonders whether his devotees could dispose of him as they see fit when they are in need, at no point does the poet declare hatred or question that god's existence or his own devotion to him.

In light of this, let us return to Kāḷamēkam. What does *his* blame-praise sound like? Here is what he says to Śiva-Vaittīcuvaraṉ ('lord of healing'):

Despite being the healer who rules over the earth,
Have you seen him heal the trouble in his throat?
If one looks at the remedy suggested by my lord from Vēḷūr[17]
Who graciously eats the feast offered by the devotees,
    It is nothing but pure soil![18]

[16]*peṟṟa pōḻtum perāta pōḻtum, pēṇi uṉ kaḻal ēttuvārkaḷ/ maṟṟ' ōr
parr'ilar eṉṟu iraṅki, mati uṭaiyavar ceykai ceyyīr;
aṟṟa pōḻtum alanta pōḻtum, āpaṟkālattu, aṭikēḷ! ummai/ oṟṟi vaittu iṅku
uṇṇalāmō? ōṇakāntintaḷi uḻīrē!*

[17]Vēḷūr is now known as Vaittīcuvaraṉ Kōyil, located nor far from Cīrkāḻi, in Tamilnadu.

[18]*maṇṭalattiṉ āḻum vayittiyar-āyt tām iruntum/ kaṇṭa viṉai tīrkkiṉṟār
kaṇṭīrō-toṇṭar*

Blame is twofold here: first, the healer is unable to heal himself, for he still has the black stain on his throat from drinking the Hālahāla poison; and second, his medicine, to cure any ailment and for all patients, is mere soil. And he gives that in exchange for food offered by the devotees. Given that the poet has elsewhere spoken of the exploit of drinking poison without which the world would have been annihilated (see v. 126 below), we know that the first part of the verse is not real criticism by any means. As for the second 'insult', the soil seems to be a reference to *purṟu-maṇ* (literally, 'soil from the termite mound'), which is traditionally used for healing. So this acceptance of the devotees' humble offering despite being a god and delivering them from their illnesses through the distribution of a natural remedy show that Kāḷamēkam was not in reality mocking his favourite deity.[19]

---

viruntaip pārtt' uṇṭ' aruḷum vēḷūr eṉ nātar/ maruntaip pārttāl cutta maṇ! 120

[19]The poet continues to laugh at the same Śiva in another verse by means of a *śleṣa*, a verse in which he does not spare any of the deities:

vātakkālan tamakku, maittuṉarkku nīriḷiv'ām!
pētap peruv ayiṟām piḷḷaitaṉaik − kōtak kēḷ
vanta viṉai tīrkka vakaiy aṟiyār vēḷūrar
enta viṉai tīrppār ivar? 122

He from Vēḷūṟ himself has windy humour/ wind for feet [while dancing];
[his] brother-in-law (Viṣṇu) has diabetes/has descended into water;
His son (Gaṇeśa) has an incongruously big belly!
He does not know the means to cure the troubles that affect his kindred!
 —which [of our] trouble will he solve?

Let us now look at a couple of verses where bold insult is offered to a deity, in a classic example of a *nindā-stuti*, the object of which is Muruka<u>n</u>:

The father (Śiva) eats by begging;
the mother (Devī) is a dark-skinned woman from the mountains;[20]
The incomparable uncle (Viṣṇu) is a thief of butter kept in pots
    suspended in a hoop;
The flat-footed elder brother has a big belly:
These are the esteemed glories of six-faced Muruka<u>n</u>![21]

Nothing here seems to hint at the existence of a *śleṣa*. Kāḷamēkam openly makes fun of Muruka<u>n</u>'s begging, wildness, thieving, and unseemly relatives, and even sarcastically remarks that those are the god's glories, thereby insulting most of his relatives. Not that these associations truly put the poet off, but that is not the point, which is rather to express his love, masquerading it as mockery. He could be empathizing with Muruka<u>n</u> for his bad luck. In another verse, the poet presents a Śiva who is not quite as much the beaten-up victim that we met above, but rather a perpetrator of violence:

> O master who are sitting virtuously on this land!
> Will the blame of
>   killing the death god,
>   Kāma,
>   and the child offered by Ci<u>r</u>uttoṇṭar

This healer can neither cure himself nor can he heal his relatives. However, since none of these are real ailments but mostly based on puns, there is no *nindā* at all here.

[20]To know more about the story around Nīli, see Shulman 1980: 195–6.

[21]*appa<u>n</u> irant' uṇṇi; āttāḷmalai nīli;/ opp' ariya māma<u>n</u> u<u>r</u>i tiruṭi; –*
cappai-k-kāl
a<u>nn</u>a<u>n</u> peruvayi<u>r</u>a<u>n</u>; ā<u>r</u>umukatta<u>n</u>ukk' iṅku/ e<u>nn</u>um perumai ivai. 145

> go away
> if you sit in state in Tiruccenkāṭu?[22]

Like many sacred places, Tiruccenkāṭu (now known as Tiruccenkōṭu), too, has the reputation of removing one's sins, but will it remove those of the lord who removes others' sins? The poet's humour and playfulness unfolds as he describes Śiva as 'sitting virtuously' at that place while his behaviour elsewhere is less than righteous or honourable. Kāḷamēkam repeats this kind of accusation in v. 117, but he does not seem to genuinely question or blame him, which is precisely the point of a *nindā-stuti*. As Nayar (1992: 74fn25) has pointed out, the gods were far too superior to be affected, let alone diminished, by such playful poems.

Among the verses that we have seen so far, especially in this section on bhakti verses, many were dedicated to the local deities, who are great gods like Śiva and Viṣṇu—known as transcendental deities in the sacred texts, such as the Upaniṣads and the Purāṇas—enshrined in a temple in this world. Singing about them itself comprises a key subgenre among the Āḻvārs and Nāyaṉmārs, something that could have spurred their poetic activity in the first place. Such verses have been referred to as 'temple poems', which abide by a few unwritten sets of rules. Let us now see how Kāḷamekam deals with the subgenre.

---

[22]*kālaṉaiyum kāmaṉaiyum kāṭṭu ciṟuttoṇṭar taru/ pālaṉaiyum koṉṟa pali pōmō? – cīlamuṭaṉ*
nāṭṭilē viṟṟirunta nātarē! nīr tiruccen-/kāṭṭilē viṟṟiruntakkāl! 140

A Pilgrim's Progress

While describing the contents of Ālvār poetry, Friedhelm Hardy (2001 [1983]: 270-272) refers to six characteristic features, which I find best applied to the temple poems, i.e. verses dedicated to a local god, whether Śiva or Viṣṇu: (1) ornamentation (with formulaic expressions); (2) paraphrases (to refer to the enshrined god); (3) allusions to events from Itihāsas and/or Purāṇas; (4) attributions (non-epic/non-Purāṇic attributes); (5) references to temples; and (6) descriptions of temples (and not merely a passing mention). How far Kāḷamēkam follows his bhakti predecessors is one of the questions that I will tackle here.

To begin with, marking the geographic location of a person seems to have been of some importance to our poet, for he often mentions a person along with the place that they belong to, e.g. the devadasis like Cōmi of Tiruvārūr (v.182) or Kalaicci from Kamalai-Tiruvārūr (v. 183). He seems to associate people and places, and to recognize the one with the help of the other. Naming and shaming also become more effective when he tags someone geographically, at a time when towns and their population were relatively small, and most people would know a fellow villager or townsman and instantly recognize them through the poet's words: thus, 'Campantāṇṭār from the eternal, sacred Tiruvaṇṇāmalai' (v.47) would have been easily identifiable to everyone in and around that town in his days. For Kāḷamēkam, naming and tagging are perhaps a practice, or even a habit, that he acquired while composing temple poems. Whatever the origins and reasons of such a practice, our poet mentions over forty temple-towns (or simply towns with temples), mostly (but not only) of a Śaiva affiliation in his verses, although not all of them deal with any of the gods per se. But in this section, let us read a few of Kālamēkam's temple poems and see how he understands this subgenre. Here is a simple one, with a *śleṣa* on the word *ālaṅkuṭiyāṉ*, which means both 'he from Ālaṅkuṭi/Ālam town' and 'he who will not drink poison':

Who said that he from Ālaṅkuṭi (*ālaṅkuṭiyāṉ*),
he who consumed the Hālahāla poison,
did not drink poison (*ālaṅkuṭiyāṉ*)?
>   If he had not drunk poison (*ālaṅkuṭiyāṉ*),
>   would the people of the world not have died?[23]

Kālamēkam ties here the Purāṇic story to the Sthalapurāṇa, almost in an *ākṣepa-samādhāna* ('objection – answering') method used in traditional debates, commentaries, and so forth, in which an opponent's objections are answered. Here, he responds to doubters and naysayers by pointing out that they would not be alive to question Śiva's act of protection had he not performed it to begin with. And while the poet is not explicit about his praise, he defends his favourite god, and most definitely recommends that everyone should feel gratitude for such a magnanimous, selfless act.[24]

---

[23]*ālaṅkuṭiyāṉai, ālālam uṇṭāṉai/ ālaṅ kuṭiyāṉ eṉr' ār coṉṉār? – ālaṅ kuṭiyāṉēyāyir kuvalayattōr ellām/ maṭiyārō maṇ-mītilē?* 126

[24]We saw that this verse incorporates a *śleṣa* on the word *ālaṅkuṭiyāṉ*, with *ālaṅkuṭi* referring to the town as well as to the act of drinking poison. Known as Irumpūḷai to the Nāyaṉmārs, this place has been celebrated by Campantar (2.36) as well as Appar (6.51.6). Ālaṅkuṭi may already have been a popular name at that time, possibly a reference to an abundance of banyan (*ālam*) trees

If we look back at Hardy's list of features, this verse contains Purāṇic allusions, but virtually nothing of the others, for Kāḷamēkam has privileged in this case the topic of drinking the poison and the pun that he could produce thanks to the town's name.[25] Indeed, most temple poems by Kāḷamēkam have a shade

---

in that part of the world. And then it may have come to be associated with the Purāṇic episode of Śiva drinking the poison due to the possibility of making that pun and, thus, creating a new Sthalapurāṇa for the place. Whichever way, Campantar *does* refer to this episode in the very first verse of his decade (2.36.1).

[25]Our poet can also infuse humour and *śleṣa* into a Sthalapurāṇa used in a verse. In the following one, he draws a brief portrait of Mīnākṣī's life using puns related to domesticated bovids:

> *māṭṭu-k-kōṉ taṅkai maturai viṭṭut tillai-nakar*
> *āṭṭu-k-kōṉukkup peṇṭ' āyiṉāḷ-kēṭṭ' ilaiyō?*
> *kuṭṭi maṟikkav oru kōṭṭ' āṉaiyum peṟṟāḷ*
> *kaṭṭi maṇic ciṟṟiṭaicci kāṇ.* 104

The sister of the cowherd (*māṭṭu-k-kōṉ*, Kṛṣṇa) left Maturai
and became the wife of shepherd (*āṭṭu-k-kōṉ*)/ the lord of the
    dance
    from the city of Tillai (Śiva-Naṭarāja)—
    haven't you heard?
The cowherdess/woman with a thin waist adorned with jewels
even gave birth to an owl[-like child]/ single-tusked elephant
    (Gaṇeśa),
    So as to stop the [goat's] kids/
    So that [we] knock on [our] temples and bend [in worship],
        see!

The poet hints here at the Sthapurāṇas of two sacred places, namely, Madurai and Chidambaram. The first place is associated with Mīnākṣī, whose brother is said to be Aḷakar-Viṣṇu. The second location is Tillai-Chidambaram, associated with the dancing Śiva-Naṭarāja. Although not composing a conventional temple poem, Kāḷamēkam uses different Sthalapurāṇic stories in his verse.

of *nindā* (e.g. 159, 122 [quoted above]), sometimes mingled with *śleṣa*.[26] As a matter of fact, Kālamēkam does not often expand upon describing the location, whether with formulaic clichés or otherwise. When he is not being sarcastic or mocking (and even when he is!), he is more likely to narrate a Purāṇic event (such as Śiva's destruction of the three cities) more than a Sthalapurāṇic one, and couple it with a poetic device like *śleṣa*.

However, Kālamēkam has composed a few verses that do echo some of the bhakti poets, although their verses do not fit Hardy's more general description either: making lists.

kūṭal, puṉavāyil, kurrālam, āppaṉūr,
ēṭaka(m), nelvēli, irāmēcam, āṭāṉai,
teṉ paraṅkuṉram, culiyal, teṉ tirupputtūr, kāci,
vaṉkoṭuṅkuṉram pūvaṇam. 169

Kūṭal, Puṉavāyil, Kurrālam, Āppaṉūr,
Ēṭaka(m), Nelvēli, Irāmēcam, Āṭāṉai,
beautiful paraṅkuṉram, Culiyal, beautiful Tirupputtūr, Kāci,
the mighty Koṭuṅkuṉram, Pūvaṇam.

Fitting a string of names into a verse (only adding one gap-filler, *teṉ*, twice) while also respecting the metrical rules is no mean task, although Kālamēkam is not the only one nor the first to achieve this. Some of the bhakti poets have done so, and none better than Campantar, who dedicated a whole decade for the purpose (known as the 'Tiru Kṣettirakkōvai'):

---

[26]For example, v. 162 lists all the ailments that afflict the lord, and the second way of interpreting it lists his qualities. And v. 131 can be read as describing either Raṅganātha or a gem.

Ārūr, Tillai-y-ampalam, Vallam, Nallam, northern
    Kāñcī[puram], Accirupākkam, good
Kūrūr, Kuṭavāyil, Kuṭantai, Veṇṇi, Kaḷippālai surrounded by
    the seas, southern Kōṭi,
the great Ninriyūr with paddy-fields where water flows,
    Kunriyūr, Kurukāvaiyūr, Nāraiyūr, Pērūr
With extensive woodlands, Neyttānam with good, extensive
    paddy-fields:
Rave about the great places of the moon-bearing [Śiva]!
    Tirumurai 2.39.1[27]

The difference, however, is that he adds a few formulaic expressions to describe some of the places, although perhaps only to get some breathing space in the verse. More importantly, the last part of the verse exhorts the audience to engage in an act of worship (here, remembering and reciting these place names). And perhaps true to his nature and style, Kāḷamēkam does not even bother to make a sentence that would incorporate this list—let alone add a word of salutation or exhortation—so that unless one knows what these places are, it is not easy to guess the logic behind the choice, or even to figure out that the poet is naming the Śaiva temple towns of the Pāṇḍya land.

In a slightly different tone, our poet names the best things about the different neighbourhoods in the Kanchipuram area:

[27]*ārūr, tillai-y-ampalam, vallam, nallam, vaṭa kacciyum, accirupākkam, nalla*

kūrūr, kuṭavāyil, kuṭantai, veṇṇi, kaṭal cūl kalippālai, teṉ kōṭi, pīṭ' ār nīr ūr vayal ninriyūr, kunriyūrum, kurukāvaiyūr, nāraiyūr, nīṭu kāṉap pērūr, nal nīḻvayal neyttāṉamum, pitarrāy piraicūṭi-taṉ pēr iṭamē.
(*Tirumurai* 2.39.1)

> O father!
> Greens from Kumarakōṭṭam,
> Bittergourd from Cevilimēṭu,
> The pond water from Parutti,
> The wind at the copper gates [of the temple],
> The penance under the Śiva shrine,
> The leaping of the Karumāṟi [water]
> Are delightful to everyone[28]

Although not by any means a conventional 'temple poem', this verse does give us some idea about the landscape in which the Śiva temple in Kanchipuram is located, and is also reminiscent of a verse by Tirunāvukkaracar, who seeks to give material examples of how soothing Śiva's feet are.[29] Therefore, Kāḷamēkam does show influence of his bhakti predecessors, but he also adapts his style according to his own wishes and needs. And there is something else, perhaps an extension of temple poems, also rather rare among the Āḻvārs and the Nāyaṉmārs: poems in praise of the temple deities during their procession. These verses echo the *ulā* genre in Tamil, in which a hero in a procession attracts women, who fall in love with him at first sight (see fn 32). Verses

---

[28]*appā kumarakōṭṭak kīrai, cevilimēṭ-/ṭup pākaṟkāy, paruttik kuḷanīr — ceppu-vā-*
cal kāṟṟu, kampatt' aṭiyil tavam, karumā-/ṟip pāyccal yārkkum iṉitu.
(45)
[29]*mācil vīṇaiyum mālai matiyamum/ vīcu teṉṟalum vīṅk' iḷavēṉilum*
mūcu vaṇṭ' aṟai poykaiyum pōṉratē/ īcaṉ entaiy iṉaiy aṭi nīḻalē.
(*Tirumuṟai* 5.90.1)

The shade at the pair of feet of the lord, my father, is like:
flawless *vīṇā* music, the evening moon,
the blowing breeze, the abundance of early spring,
and a pond swarming with buzzing bees.

in honour of processional deities may not be very prevalent among the earlier bhakti poets because a temple having both a main deity (*mūlamūrti*) installed and a processional icon (*utsavamūrti*), and taking the latter out during festivals and other special occasions were practices that became more established in the second millennium.[30] Since Kāḷamēkam seems to have gone from one temple-town to another,[31] it is not a surprise that he should have witnessed and enjoyed these festive occasions, out of which verses infused with his characteristic humour came:

> [This] Perumāḷ(Viṣṇu) is a good Perumāḷ;
> [and] his festival is a good festival too.
> [But] since Perumāḷ did not stay put where he was,
> a kite is carrying him away, alas![32]

This is clearly a verse that the poet sang during the *Garuḍa sevai* (procession during which Viṣṇu is carried on the back of a representation of his vehicle, Garuḍa the kite),[33] possibly at the Varadarāja temple in Kanchipuram (Puliyūr 2010: 71). During this procession, Viṣṇu is taken around riding his kite, which Kāḷamēkam humorously describes as an abduction of

---

[30]There are exceptions, of course. To know more details on this topic, see Orr 2004.

[31]A few other verses also apparently deal with processional deities, e.g. v. 101, 110, 134, 138, and 139.

[32]*perumāḷum nalla perumāḷavar-tan/ tiru-nāḷum nulla tiru-nāḷ-perumāḷ*
irunt' iṭattil cummāy irāmaiyināl, aiyō!/ parunt'eṭuttup pōkitē! pār!
107

[33]Deities are taken around in processions, sometimes mounted on different types of vehicles, in this case, Garuḍa, Viṣṇu's favourite vehicle. For more on temple festivals, see Orr 2004.

the god as he left the safety of his temple. A few other verses express his joy at witnessing such a procession. However, his (good?) humour disappears the moment he turns from spectator to actor:

O Lord [Viṣṇu] of Kayirrāru, which bears the scent of swathes
    of palms!
Great sinner! Listen!
As for the time, it is over sixteen *nālikai*s into the night[34] at this
    moment!
Apart from breaking my shoulder, you also made me carry the
    weight of the priest!
Who will bear you from tomorrow onwards?
May your temple be ruined forever![35]

Whatever wooden frame was used to bear the deities during the procession has traditionally been carried on the shoulders by men (either trained ones, or even visiting men in the absence of trained carriers). And sometimes added to their weight is that of a priest sitting or standing on that frame along with the icon of the deity. In this verse, which truly brings out the physical pain of the poet, and his ensuing fury, he is seen cursing a god, and in the process, it confirms something that we suspected about him: Kāḷamēkam is very susceptible to getting angry when he is directly affected by someone else's words or actions, even it is

---

[34]One *nālikai* roughly corresponds to twenty-four minutes, and thus 16 *nālikai*s × 24 = 384 minutes = 6.4 hours. If we calculate nightfall from sunset (roughly 6 o'clock in the evening), then our poet had been made to carry that heavy frame till past midnight.

[35]*pāḷai maṇam kamalukiṉra kayirrārrup perumāḷē paḷikārā kēḷ/
vēḷaiy eṉrāl ivvēḷai patiṉāru nāḷikaikku mēl āyirru eṉ
tōḷai muṛittatum aṉri nampiyāṉaiyum kūṭac cumakkac ceytāy
nāḷai iṉi yār cumappār eṉṉāḷum uṉ kōyil nācantāṉē.* 200

a god's (with perhaps the exception of Śiva—whom he does not curse despite using sarcasm and insults when speaking of/to him—and Śiva's family). This is unlike the practice of the bhakti poets: for example, while the Āḻvārs definitely composed *nindā-stuti*s, they have not hurled such virulent curses. The belief is that the temple lay in ruins as a result of his words.

Kāḷamēkam thus differs from the bhakti poets. He also does so because he celebrates more than one god, which, in turn, allows him to be less considerate towards the ones who are not his absolute favourites. So while Kāḷamēkam composes verses on various deities (e.g. Śiva, Gaṇeśa, Viṣṇu, and so forth), not all gods are equal in his eyes.

Establishing the Supremacy of the Favourite God: *Nindā* and *Stuti*

Among the deities that he sings about, whether in direct praise, direct abuse, or in a neutral way, Śiva is the poet's favourite choice, although he does seem to cherish Devī as well. On more than one occasion, either consciously or unconsciously, he establishes this deity's supremacy, especially as opposed to Viṣṇu-Nārāyaṇa's. In the process, just as the bhakti poets did,[36] he belittles one god to elevate another.

[36]See, for example, Tirumaḻicai Āḻvār's verse as he establishes his own favourite deity as the Supreme Being: *aṟiyār camaṇar ayarttār pavuttar/ ciṟiyār civappaṭṭār ceppil veṟiyāya/ māyavaṉai mālavaṉai mātavaṉai ēttār/iṉavarē ātalāl iṉṟu!* 'The Jains do not know [the truth], the Buddhists have forgotten [it],/ Śiva's priests are insignificant people. To state [the truth], those who do not praise the fragrant Dark One, Māl-Viṣṇu, Mādhava are therefore base people now' (*Nāṉmukaṉ Tiruvantāti* 6)

Our poet is well-aware of the goings-on in the temples, including fights between Śaivas and Vainṣavas, as is clear from the following verse, set in Śrīraṅgam, the most important Śrīvaiṣṇava temple, and the nearby Śaiva temple-town, Tiruvāṉaikkā:

cīraṅkattārum tiruvāṉaikkāvārum
pōr aṅkam ākap poruvat' ēṉ? ōraṅkaḷ
vēṇṭām! itu eṉṉa viparam teriyātō?
āṇṭāṉum tātaṉum āṉāl? 143

Why do the people from Śrīraṅgam and those from Tiruvāṉaikkā
compete as if in a battlefield?
No need for partiality.
Don't you know the details?
If ruler (āṇṭāṉ) and servant (tātaṉ) they be, [fights are bound to
    happen] (emphasis mine)

This verse is a little enigmatic because it is elliptical towards the end. Puliyūr (2010: 93) claims that the words *āṇṭāṉ* ('ruler') means 'those who have been ruled over by the lord', and *tātaṉ* ('servant') refers to the priests in the Śiva and Viṣṇu temples, respectively. He therefore concludes that Kāḷamēkam is insinuating that the latter are inferior to the former. Śrītaraṉ (2013: 203–4), who comes across as being partial to the Vaiṣṇava side, adds that the Vaiṣṇavas are known as *tātaṉ/dāsa* because they seek surrender in God, although he offers the same explanation as Puliyūr. However, this interpretation cannot be verified. For one, while the *Madras Tamil Lexicon* defines *tātaṉ* as 'slave, devotee' and *āṇṭāṉ* as 'master, ruler', there is no definite indication that either word refers to priests. Piḷḷai (2020 [2006]: 150) goes a step further and believes that *āṇṭāṉ* and *tātaṉ* refer to Śiva and Viṣṇu, respectively. However, although the Śrīvaiṣṇavas refer to themselves as being the servants of Rāmānuja, of the Lord, of any Śrīvaiṣṇava, not all of them use the suffix *tātaṉ/dāsaṉ,* just as some of them used the suffix *āṇṭāṉ* (e.g. Mutaliyāṇṭāṉ). The *Mañcari* (p. 231) also offers an alternative interpretation to the line: both Śaivas and Vaiṣṇavas believe in the existence of a Master (i.e. God) and of a servant (i.e. the individual soul), and this verse shows the existence of different souls and the superiority of one of them (i.e. God).[37] But this does not help with the understanding of what is left unsaid (i.e. 'fights are bound to happen' in Puliyūr's [2010: 93–94] understanding). Keeping all this in mind, we might still agree that Kāḷamēkam did state the inferiority of the Vaiṣṇava priests vis-à-vis the Śaiva priests in light of his other verses, some of which directly or indirectly establish the superiority of Śiva over Viṣṇu-Nārāyaṇa and others criticize the priests in the Vaiṣṇava temples (e.g. v. 215), never the Śaiva ones.

One way in which Kāḷamēkam seeks to establish Śiva's superiority over Viṣṇu-Nārāyaṇa is by pointing out that Śiva is devoid of birth and death, while Viṣṇu has had ten or more births. We already have come across a verse that introduces this idea: 'You (Viṣṇu) had ten births; Śiva has had none' (v. 137, see above). That verse clearly played with irony, with greatness being measured by the number of births that one has taken. The following poem—apparently dedicated to Śiva—seems to follow suit:

[37]Moreover, in a footnote, the editor of the *Mañcari* (p. 231) states that some people read *āṇṭāṉ* as *āṇṭi* (which refers to either a class of non-brahmin Śaivas or to Śaiva mendicants according to the MTL) and that this reading was not correct.

tantai piṟant' iṟavāt taṉmaiyiṉāl, taṉ māmaṉ
vantu piṟant' iṟakkum vaṉ/vaṇmaiyiṉāl – munt' oru nāḷ
vīṇ ikku vēḷaiy erittāṉ makaṉ māmaṉ
kāṇikku vant' iruntāṉ kāṇ. 146

Due to his father's (Śiva's) nature of not being born and not
    dying,
due to the *generosity* of his uncle (Viṣṇu) in taking births and
    dying,
the son of [Śiva] who once burned Kāma—who has a useless
    sugarcane bow—
has come and stayed for the sake of his uncle's property, see!
    (emphasis mine)

As per Śrītaraṉ's (2013: 72) explanations, since
Śiva has no property (not being part of this mortal
world) as opposed to Viṣṇu who does (since he has
taken so many avatāras here), and since the latter's
son Kāma is dead (killed by Śiva), Gaṇeśa—Śiva's
son and Viṣṇu's nephew—has come to claim the
hereditary rights (*kāṇi*) from his uncle. We see how the
poet plays with Purāṇic narratives (the divine family
tree, Kāma's 'dying' at Śiva's hand, and so forth) and
localizes them. He may have done this in order to
right a perceived wrong, for both Śrītaraṉ (2013: 72)
and Puliyūr (2010: 95) suggest that he composed this
verse in pique after the Vaiṣṇavas in Śrīraṅgam had
applied the Vaiṣṇava *tirumaṇ* mark on the forehead
of a Gaṇeśa icon. In short: Kāḷamēkam uses the
argument of Viṣṇu's many births as opposed to Śiva's
'birthlessness', as well as the death of the former's son
at the hands of the latter,[38] to establish the mortality
of the one and the endless power of the other.

---

[38]In another verse, Kāḷamēkam almost gleefully describes Śrī-
Lakṣmī's grief at learning about her son Kāma's death:

Elsewhere too, the modern *kiḷavis*—many of which, as mentioned above, might be based on older texts such as the *Mañjari*—often mention how Kālamēkam feels provoked when someone claims Viṣṇu-Nārāyaṇa's superiority. The following verse is another such example: no one could assert Viṣṇu's superiority simply because he is in a reclining position with his feet pointing at the dancing Naṭarāja-Śiva inside the Chidambaram temple, technically a posture indicating the former's lack of respect towards the latter for the following reason.

If you think that Māl-Nārāyaṇa has extended [His] feet to the
    northern side
towards him of the Little Chamber (Naṭarāja-Śiva), who is
    suitable for dancing:
there is nothing to blame in a bull, which grew tired
of carrying him who conquered the three cities that he burnt.[39]

cutta pārkaṭaliṉ naṭuviṉil tūḷi tōṉriya aticayam atu kēḷ!
mattaka kariyai urittavaṉ mītu mataṉ porut' aḷintiṭu(m) mārram
vittaka kamalai ceviyuṟa kēṭṭāḷ: viḻuntu, nontu, ayarnt' aḻutu, ēṅki
kaittala malarāl mārp'uṟa puṭaittāḷ! eḻuntatu kalavaiyiṉ cem tūḷ. 31

Hear about the marvel of dust appearing in the midst of the
    pure milk ocean!
The great Kamalā heard the news of Kāma getting destroyed
    while fighting with [Śiva] who skinned
the elephant with protuberant temples: she fell; suffering
    [greatly], she fainted; she cried; she wailed;
she beat [her] breasts with the lotus in [her] hands! [And thus]
    rose the red dust of the perfumed paste!

[39]*āṭṭukku icaintavar ampalavāṇar avarkku etirē/ nīṭṭirru māl vaṭa*
pāḷiṉil kāl eṉa nī niṉaiyēl
cūṭṭ'uṟṟa mup-p-uram cerravar tammaic cumantu alutta/ māṭṭukku
eṉṉōv iṭam kāl nīṭṭal colla vaḻakku illaiyē. 95

The tiff between Śaivas and Vaiṣṇavas in Chidambaram is notorious and goes back many centuries. If the proximity of the two temples in Śrīraṅgam and Tiruvāṉaikkā is the root cause of the constant bickering mentioned by Kāḷamēkam in v. 143, then what to say of Chidambaram, where the most important Śaiva shrine contains within it one of the sacred shrines (*divyadeśam*) for the Vaiṣṇavas?[40] No wonder Kāḷamēkam felt compelled to pronounce his own opinion on the issue, and he does so by equating Viṣṇu with a bull, as the poet claims—no doubt based on mythological narratives—that he took this animal form so that Śiva could ride him on his mission to destroy Tripura. This image pleases the poet so well that he repeats it in many verses (e.g. v. 100, v. 149, v. 154), so much so that on one occasion, he attributes all of Viṣṇu's exploits to Śiva's bull, thereby transferring the glory to its 'master', namely, Śiva at Tiruvīḻimiḻalai:

> *kāḷāl paṭi aḷakkum, kaṇ iṭantu pūcikkum,*
> *cēlāṅka maṭam ām, ciṅkam ām, pāl ākum*
> *āḻi appilē tuyilum, aivarkkut tūtu ākum,*
> *vīḻiyappar ēṟum viṭai.* 130

> The bull ridden by Vīḻiyappar
>   measures the earth with its feet;
>   worships by scooping out its eyes;
>   becomes a fish, a tortoise, a lion;

[40]It is believed that a Śaiva Cōḻa king even threw the icon of Viṣṇu-Govindarāja that was enshrined in the temple complex, which was reinstated later. It is worth noting that even today, staunch Śrīvaiṣṇavas would hide a part of their face to avoid seeing/being seen by Śiva-Naṭarāja on their way to the Govindarāja-Viṣṇu shrine.

sleeps on the water of the milky ocean;
becomes a messenger for five people.[41]

It seems that Kālamēkam does not just believe Viṣṇu to be a bull that Śiva rode during the Tripura battle, but in fact replaces Nandin—the bull traditionally considered Śiva's vehicle,[42] whom he does not mention to my knowledge—with Nārāyaṇa the bull. This is interesting, since Kālamēkam is also aware of the other two variants of the Śiva-Tripurāntaka story, for he mentions that Śiva destroyed the three cities by laughing ('he burned down the cities by laughing' *cirittu puram erittān* v. 147; 'you displayed your teeth' *pallai tirantu viṭṭīr* v. 151) and that Viṣṇu became Śiva's arrow that destroyed those cities ('He became [your] arrow' *ampākiṉāṉ* v.158). What matters here is that the Vaiṣṇavas would consider such equations of Viṣṇu with Śiva's bull as a considerable insult, which is likely Kālamēkam's aim too. Thus the *nindā* of one god becomes the *stuti* of another, and this berating of Viṣṇu does not necessarily come across as following the principle of *nahi nindā*, in which the insult of one person is *not* meant to degrade them, but rather, just to extol another.[43] Another interesting thing about this

---

[41]Viṣṇu as Vāmana-Trivikrama measured the worlds; in the Sthalapurāṇa of Tiruvīlimilalai, Viṣṇu plucks out his eyes to worship Śiva; Viṣṇu's avatāras ('descents') include the fish, the tortoise and the [man-]lion; he sleeps on the milk ocean, and as Kṛṣṇa, he served as a messenger for the five Pāṇḍava brothers.

[42]To know more about Nandin, see Orblskaya and Orelskaya 1997.

[43]This comes from the maxim *na hi nindā nindyaṃ ninditum prayujyate kiṃ tarhi ninditāditarat praśaṃsitum* 'Blame is not employed in order to blame something that is blameworthy, but rather to

verse is that among events mentioned in the Itihāsas and the Purāṇas, we find here one that is specific to this Tiruvīḻimiḻalai temple: finding one lotus short of a thousand that he used for his daily worship, Viṣṇu scooped out one of his eyes à la Kaṇṇappa Nāyaṉār to replace the missing flower. The poet thus customizes this verse for this specific temple.

Apart from Viṣṇu, no other deity or worshipper of a different sect is attacked by Kālamēkam, not the Buddhists, nor the Jains, although the impaling of the latter is casually mentioned in v. 41. It is clear that the Buddhists and Jains are a spent force by Kālamēkam's time, and that the real rivals are the 'opponent others', viz., the Vaiṣṇavas, whom the poet tries to shame and/or dismiss by belittling their god, while still praising Viṣṇu elsewhere. The two activities are apparently not mutually exclusive for our poet.

---

praise something other than that' (tr. Jacob 1909, vol. 2: 41).

Conclusion

KĀLAMĒKAM WAS A MAN of his times: he did not really question the social setup, he took his food seriously, he loved the company of women, although he often expresses his contempt for them (especially since he seems to have frequented one type of women more than others). However, he was by no means an ordinary man, for his poetic genius shines in many of his verses. And perhaps that awareness aggravated his short temper, for he may have expected people to know, understand, and appreciate his genius. When that kind of welcome was not forthcoming, pain and bitterness seem to have poured forth in words, often disguised as anger. If indeed Kāḷamēkam was the son of a Śrīvaiṣṇava cook who had moved from rural Tirumōkūr in the south to the mainstream Śrīvaiṣṇava fortress Śrīraṅgam, he may not have been as respected as an urbane son of a scholar would have been, for example. If he had indeed 'converted' to Śaivism, and that too, for the sake of a devadasi, as the hagiography-biography states, then the scandal and its repercussions can very well be imagined. That could have further embittered a proud yet sensitive person like our poet and alienated him from the Vaiṣṇavas. Was he even estranged from his family for that reason, since he never seems to mention any family members, except perhaps in one verse (v. 6; see Chapter 2, section titled 'Kālamēkam's Values and Overview')? Was pride a mask behind which he concealed his vulnerability? All that we know for sure is what the poet proclaims about himself, presuming that it is the truth, and also perhaps everything that can be read between the lines, within reasonable limits.

As for Kālamēkam the devotee and/or the 'devotional' poet, we have seen that he was definitely conversant with the works of the Tamil bhakti poets, although he does not necessarily follow them at all times. Among the 'bhakti' verses that he has composed, many take the form of a *nindā-stuti*, mostly directed at Śiva, whom he declares through many verses as the supreme god, higher even than Viṣṇu, who is merely his bull-vehicle. And there is very little in terms of emotion in Kālamēkam's poetry, especially since his bhakti seems to be expressed through sarcasm and criticism, albeit fake at times (depending on the individual verse). Also, while he mentions many temple-towns—which he seems to have visited— he does not really compose what could be termed 'temple poems', with all the features that we discussed earlier. Furthermore, it is perhaps worth mentioning that Kālamēkam does not seem to identify with any group of devotees. He does not speak of himself as wishing to worship or worshipping along with other devotees (if at all he mentions his worshipping any god in the first place!), something that the Āḻvārs, for example, longed to do. He does not worship the other devotees either, which is a flagship feature of the bhakti poets. The later Āḻvārs, for example, valued association and devotion to the devotees of God: in his *Amalaṉ Āti Pirāṉ,* Tiruppāṇālvār claims in his very first verse that Nārāyaṇa made him belong to his devotees; Toṇṭaraṭippoṭi Āḻvār has a nom de plume that means 'dust at the feet of the devotees', and we can provide more such examples. Kāḷamēkam, however, comes across as a loner, perhaps not a devotee fundamentally, but a talented poet who was devoted to a few gods, mainly Śiva and Devī, whom he visited in the different temples, perhaps while being on the lookout for a potential patron and a living.

Now, to return to Zvelebil's (1974: 53) claim that Kāḷamēkam was 'the only Tamil writer of the past who can claim the name of satirist!': while it may not be true that our poet is the only one who deserves to be recognized for the quality of his satire, he was definitely one of the earliest and best examples of what Tamil satire looks like. Many are the forms and uses of his satirical words: they take the form of derision, which he uses to laugh in a good-natured way at bad cooks or to bring down pretentious rivals. Sometimes, his satirical words take the form of invectives, hurled at the perceived offender, curses aimed at harming them. How much of this is to teach the others to rectify their errors is a matter of debate, for our poet seems content to jeer at the others or simply vent. Women tend to fare relatively worse than men in Kāḷamēkam's satire, a phenomenon observed throughout the world because they are 'convenient scapegoats [. . . and because] satire enables men to express resentment they feel when confronted by any display of female power' (Hodgart 2002: 59). Kāḷamēkam does seem to have an ambiguous relationship with the second sex, especially when confronted with the kind of women who tend to be more independent (although definitely not emancipated in a society rigidly established by patriarchy) than the married woman inside home. Even gods are not spared by Kālamēkam, as we saw, as his verses poke fun even at his favourite god, Śiva and his wife, as he speaks to and of them as an equal. But the bitterness that characterizes his satirical verses are usually not present in his 'bhakti' ones. The latter, which mimic the bhakti verses of the Tamil saint-poets—whom he knew well—do not entirely follow the relevant conventions, as mentioned above. However, his parody cannot entirely hide his fondness—devotion even—for the very gods whom he playfully berates by means of the *nindā-stuti*.

Finally, whatever he may have been and however he may have lived, Kālamēkam has caught the imagination of many generations of poets and common people alike. And this is perhaps why another poet, Paṭikkācup Pulavar (given in Nāyakar 1927: 26) declares in his *cīṭṭuk kavi* ('epistle . . . written in verse' MTL) that he was born on this earth for the sake of singing satirical verses like Kālamēkam.[1] Another poet, Aṭṭāvatāni Āti Caravaṇapperumāḷ Kavirāyar (quoted in Aruṇācalam 1944: 28), calls himself 'the delightful poet Avatāni caravaṇapperumāḷ, a Kālamēkam who fully drinks up the oceans of grammar and literature and belches!'[2] It is not surprising that this name should be sometimes conferred as a title upon poets whose style were similar to Kālamēkam's. For example, a twentieth-century poet called Ananta Kiruṣṇaiyaṅkār was given the title 'Abhinava Kālamēkam' (the modern Kālamēkam) by none other than U. Vē. Cāminātaiyar.[3] It is as if

---

[1] *kāḷamēkam pōla vacai pāṭa yāmum ik kāciniyil avatarittōm.*

[2] *ilakkaṇa ilakkiya kaṭalai muḻutum kuṭitt' ēppam iṭu kāḷamēkam, iniya kavi avatāni caravaṇap perumāḷ.*

[3] It would seem that U. Vē. Cāminātaiyar wrote a Preface

Kālamēkam has become a yardstick for measuring excellence in certain types of poetry-making, satire, wordplay, and so forth. Many poets have sought to imitate him as well. Besides the fact that imitation is the best form of flattery, the very fact that Kālamēkam is still remembered and much better known than all these poets allows us to confidently affirm that his poetry has withstood the test of time.

Apart from that, one medium that has steadily grown in importance and influence in the Indian subcontinent throughout the twentieth century is the silver screen, and our poet has left his mark there too. I have mentioned in Chapter 1 that one of his verses (v. 66) was used to write a song in a Tamil film (see Chapter 1, fn 42) by the famous poet-lyricist Kaṇṇatācaṉ in 1963. Additionally, in a Tamil biopic dedicated to Kālidāsa—named *Mahākavi Kāḷitās* (1966), with the legendary 'Sivaji' Ganesan playing the lead role—Kaṇṇatācaṉ uses ideas and words very similar to Kālamēkam's v. 2 while verbalizing Kālidāsa's feeling of gratitude.[4] Apart from spotting the parallel

for a work (*Tiruppērai Kalampakam*) published by this poet in 1937, in which he gave him this title. I could unfortunately not verify this information because I could not access the book in question. I obtained this information from personal blogs, namely, https://oomaikkanavugal.blogspot.com/2015/12/blog-post_7.html (accessed 8 September 2023) and https://www.keetru.com/index.php/2010-06-24-04-31-11/ungal-noolagam-nov19/39095-2019-11-13-04-32-19 (accessed 6 April 2023).

[4]Please compare Kālamēkam's words from v. 2 (translated in full in the Chapter 3 section titled 'Devotional Verses'), 'the mother who placed me upon an equal seat alongside kings on white thrones' (*veḷḷai/ ariyācaṉattil aracarōṭ' eṉṉaic/ cariy ācaṉam vaitta tāy*) with Kaṇṇatācaṉ's *yār taruvār inta ariyācaṉam, puvi aracōṭu*

stories of Kālidāsa and Kālamēkam, which he used to his advantage while composing the lyrics meant for a Tamil audience, Kaṇṇatācaṉ was definitely inspired by our poet's verses as well.

Perhaps of greater importance is that a Tamil biopic of Kālamēkam was made by American director Ellis R. Dungan in 1940, with T.N. Rajarathinam Pillai, the virtuoso Nādasvaram player, essaying the role of the poet, and none other than the twentieth-century revolutionary poet Putuvai Pāratitācaṉ penning the dialogues and the lyrics. The film was a success, along with films such as the classics *Cakuntalai* and *Uttama Puttiraṉ*, all released in 1940. As if people were not satisfied with that one film, another one was made in 1978 on his life, entitled *Kavirāja Kālamēkam* by G. Or. Nathan, with the renowned playback singer T.M. Countarrājaṉ (famously known as TMS) playing the lead role. Although the writer of the screenplay of this film has used his imagination to the fullest, the very existence of the film attests to our poet's long-lasting fame, which is also widely discussed in social media, thus taking his poetry to the future generations as well.[5] And that is something that would indeed have pleased Kālamēkam.

---

eṉakkum oru cari ācaṉam? ammā! 'Who will give such a throne, an equal seat with the kings of the world? Oh mother!'

[5]Discussions about his poetry abound: see, for example, https://groups.google.com/g/friendindia/c/3CG8Kfm0Xfw/m/MpKThwZC-B4J (accessed 8 September 2023), https://groups.google.com/g/santhavasantham/c/B_QjTljPL-0/m/jGpiuBjE0yEJ (accessed 8 September 2023), or https://groups.google.com/g/mintamil/c/RJBHxg-DUxs (accessed 8 September 2023).

PLATE: The poster of the film *Kāḷamēkam* (1940)
Source: https://commons.wikimedia.org/wiki/
File:Kalamegam_poster.jpg

Bibliography

Primary Sources

Aiṅkuṟunūṟu (1920). *Eṭṭut tokaiyuḷ mūnṟāvatākiya aiṅkuṟunūṟum paḻaiya uraiyum.* Ed. by Uttamatāṉapuram Mahāmahopāttiyāya Vē. Cāminātaiyar. Ceṉṉai: Kaṇeca accukkūṭam. 2nd edition.

Āḻvār poetry. See Nālāyira Divya Prabandham.

Cittira Maṭal by Kāḷamēkam (1978). *Kāḷamēkap pulavar iyaṟṟiya cittira maṭal.* Ed. by Pulavar Cānta Cuntaraṉār. Ceṉṉai: Caiva sittānta patippuk kaḻakam.

Ciṟiya Tirumaṭal by Tirumaṅkai Āḻvār. See Nālāyira Divyaprabandham.

Irāmāvatāram by Kampaṉ (2011 [2006]). *Kamparāmāyaṇam. pālakāṇṭam (mūlamum uraiyum).* Edited and commented upon by Vai. Mu. Kōpālakiruṣṇamāccāriyār. Ceṉṉai: Umā patipppakam.

Kāḷamēkam's self-contained verses (editions)

———— (2020 [2006]). *taṉippāṭal tiraṭṭu. Mūlamum uraiyum.* Vol. 1. Ed. and Comm. by Kā. Cuppiramaṇiyap Piḷḷai. Ceṉṉai: Cāratā Patipppakam.

———— (2010). *Kāḷamēkap pulavar. taṉip pāṭalkaḷ.* Ed. by Puliyūr Kēcikaṉ. Ceṉṉai: Maṅkai Veḷiyīṭu.

———— (2013) *Kāḷamēkap pulavar taṉip pāṭalkaḷ.* Ed. and Comm. by N. Śrītaraṉ. Ceṉṉai: Kaṅkai Puttaka Nilaiyam.

———— (n.d.). *Kāḷamēkap pulavar pāṭalkaḷ.* Ed. and comm. by Ceṅkai Potuvaṉ. Ebook. https://ta.wikisource.org/

wiki/காளமேகப்_புலவர்_பாடல்கள். Accessed on 7 April 2023.

Kaliṅkattu Paraṇi by Cayaṅkoṇṭār (1923). *Kavicakkaravartti cayaṅkoṇṭār pāṭiya kaliṅkattup paraṇi, mūlamum arumporuḷviḷakkamutaliyaṉavum.* Ed. by A. Kōpālaiyaṉ. Ceṉṉai: Kamarṣiyal accukkūṭam.

Meyppāṭṭiyal. See Tolkāppiyam.

Nālāyira Divya Prabandham by the Āḻvārs. (1918). *Āḻvārkaḷ aruḷicceyta nālāyira tivyaprapantam.* Ed. by Tiruvallikkēṇi tamiḻ paṇṭitar Cē. Kiruṣṇamācāriyar. Ceṉṉai: Kaṇēca accukkūṭam.

Nāyaṉmār poetry. See Tēvāram.

Periya Purāṇam by Cēkkiḻār. (1950). *Cēkkiḻār perumāṉ aruḷiya Periya purāṇam eṉa valaṅkum tiruttoṇṭar purāṇam (paṉṉiraṇṭān tirumuṟai).* Ceṉṉai: Caiva sittānta makā camājam.

Periyāḻvār Tirumoḻi. See Nālāyira Divya Prabandham.

Pulavar Purāṇam by Taṇṭapāṇi Cuvāmikaḷ (1908). *Pulavar purāṇam.* Ceṉṉai: Ti. Mu. Centiṉāyakam Piḷḷai.

Rāmāyaṇa by Vālmīki (1933). *Śrīmadvālmīkirāmāyaṇam.* Ed. by K. Chinnaswami Sastrigal and V.H. Subrahmanya Sastri. Madras: N. Ramaratnam. 2nd edition.

Tēvāram by the Nāyaṉmārs (2007). *Digital Tēvāram: With the Complete English gloss of the Late V.M. Subramanya Ayyar (IFP) and Furnished with a Full Concordance of the Tamil Text Accompanied by 6 Hours of MP3 Audio Recordings (Illustrating all the 24 paṇ-s) Various Maps (Showing all the 274 talam-s) and Other Related Material.* Ed. by Ayyar, Subramanya, V.M., J.L. Chevillard, and S.A.S. Sarma. Paris: École française d'Extrême-Orient.

Tamiḻ Nāvalar Caritai (1916). *Tamiḻ Nāvalar Caritai.* Ed. by Cāmi Tillai Naṭēca Ceṭṭiyār. Ceṉṉai: Ci. Ku. Nārāyaṇacāmi Mutaliyār.

Tirumuṟai. See Tēvāram.

Tolkāppiyam (2014 [2008]). *Tolkāppiyam: mūlamum uraiyum.* Ed. and Comm. by Tamiḻaṇṇal. Maturai: Mīnāṭci puttaka nilaiyam.

Vinōta raca Mañcari (*Mañcari*) (1958). *Aṣṭāvatānam Vīrācāmi Ceṭṭiyār avarkaḷ iyarriya Vinōta raca Mañcari*. With a Preface by Ve. Irāmaliṅkam Piḷḷai. Cennai: Ti Liṭṭil Plavar Kampeni [LIFCO].

Secondary Sources

Anandakichenin, Suganya (2022). 'Bold and Forthright: Mapping the Evolution of Tirumaḷicai Āḻvār and His Irreverent Voice.' *The World of The Orient* 4, pp. 163–177. https://doi.org/10.15407/orientw2022.04.163.

Anandakichenin, Suganya (2024). *For the Blemishless Lord. A Study of Three Śrīvaiṣṇava Medieval Commentaries on Tiruppāṇālvār's* Amalan Āti Pirān. Beyond Boundaries Series (11). Berlin: De Gruyter.

Aruṇācalam, Mu., ed. (1944). *Kālamēkap pulavar pāṭiya Tiru Āṉaikkā Ulā: Mūlamum Kurippuraiyum*. Cokkanātapuram: Centamilk kalakam.

———— (2005 [1969]). *Tamiḷ Ilakkiya Varalāru. Patinaintām Nūrrāṇṭu*. Cennai: The Parkar.

Ben-Herut, Gil (2018). *Śiva's Saints: The Origins of Devotion in Kannada According to Harihara's Ragaḷegaḷu*. New York: Oxford University Press.

Burrow, Thomas, & M. B. Emeneau (1984). *Dravidian Etymological Dictionary*. (2nd ed.) Oxford: Clarendon Press.

Cāmiṉātaiyar, U. Vē. (1991 [1938]). *Nalluraikkōvai*. Vol. 3. Cennai: Makāmakōpāttiyāya ṭākṭar U. Vē. Cāmiṉātaiyar nūl nilaiyam.

———— (1950). *En carittiram*. Cennai: Es. Kaliyāṇacuntaraiyar.

Ceṅkuṭṭuvaṉ, Kō. (2017). *Camaṇar kaḻuvērram. Oru varalārrut tēṭal* (ebook). Cennai: Kiḷakku patippakam.

Culianu, Ioan P. (1995). 'Introduction: The Body Re-examined', in Jane Marie Law, ed., *Religious Reflections on the Human Body*. Bloomington: n.p., pp. 1–18.

Cuntaranār. See Cittira maṭal.

Dravidian Etymological Dictionary. See Burrow and Emeneau 1984.

Egendorff, Laura K., ed. (2022). *Satire*. San Diego: Greenhaven Press.

Gonda, J. (1948). 'Her begrip bhakti', in *Tijdschrift voor Philosophie* 10, pp. 607–60.

Hardy, Friedhelm (2001 [1983]). *Viraha-Bhakti: The Early History of Kṛṣṇa Devotion in South India*. New Delhi: Oxford University Press.

Hodgart, Matthew (2002). 'The Treatment of Women in Satire'. In Laura K. Egendorff, ed., *Satire*. San Diego: Greenhaven Press.

Mātavaṉ, Vē. Irā. (1983). *Cittirakavikaḷ*. Madras: International Institute of Tamil Studies.

Ñāṉacēkaraṉ, Tē. (2009). 'Cittar pāṭalkaḷil peṇ uṭal cittarippu'. *Centamiḻ* 103 (2), pp. 9–19.

Nāyakar, Pu. A. Kōvintarāja, ed. (1927). *Pala vittuvāṉkaḷiyarriya cīṭṭukkavit tiraṭṭu*. Ceṉṉai: Māraṉ accukkūṭam.

Nayar, Nancy Ann (1992). *Poetry as Theology: The Śrīvaiṣṇava Stotra in the Age of Rāmānuja*. Wiesbaden: Otto Harrassowitz Verlag.

Orblskaya, Marina V. and Marina V. Orelskaya (1997). 'Nanidkeśvara in Hindu Mythology'. *Annals of the Bhandarkar Oriental Research Institute* 78 (1/4), pp. 233–248.

Orr, Leslie C. (2004). 'Processions in the Medieval South India Temple: Sociology, Sovereignty and Soteriology'. In Jean-Luc Chevillard et al., *South-Indian Horizons: Felicitation Volume for François Gros on the Occasion of his 70th Birthday*. Pondichéry: Institut Français de Pondichéry and École Française d'Extrême Orient.

Ferro-Luzzi, Gabriella Eichinger (1986). 'Language, Thought, and Tamil Verbal Humor.' *Current Anthropology* 27 (3), pp. 265–72.

Fredrickson, Barbara L., and Tomi-Ann Roberts (1997). 'Objectification Theory: Toward Understanding Women's Lived Experiences and Mental Health Risks.' *Psychology of Women Quarterly* 21 (2), pp. 173–206. http://doi.org/10.1111/j.1471-6402.1997.tb00108.x.

Hirst, Jacqueline Suthren (2008). 'Who Are the Others? Three Moments in Sanskrit-Based Practice.' In Nile Green and Mary Searle-Chatterjee, ed., *Religion, Language, and Power*. New York: Routledge, pp. 101–22.

Irattinam, Kā. Po. (1946). 'Nakaiccuvaiyum tamililakkiyamum', *Centamil* 43 (12), pp. 229–31.

Jacob, George Andrew (1909). *A Handful of Popular Maxims Current in Sanskrit Literature*. Vol. 2. Bombay: Tukârâm Jâvajî.

Nākacuvāmi, Irā. (1976). 'Kalveṭṭil kāḷamēkam', *Kalveṭṭu* 9, pp. 39–40.

Nākarācan, Tirumēni (1967). 'Nakai'. *Centamil* 93 (2), pp. 20–27.

Nanda, Vivek et al., eds. (2004). *Chidambaram. Home of Nataraja*. Mumbai: Marg Publishers.

Neevel, Walter G. (1977). *Yāmuna's Vedānta and Pāñcarātra: Integrating the Classical and the Popular.* Missouri: University of Montana.

Orr, Leslie C. (2000). *Donors, Devotees, and Daughters of God: Temple Women in Medieval Tamilnadu*. New York: Oxford University Press.

Raman, Srilata (2022). *The Transformation of Tamil Religion: Ramalinga Swamigal (1823–1874) and Modern Dravidian Sainthood*. London: Routledge. https://doi.org/10.4324/9781315794518.

Ramanujan, A.K., Velcheru Narayana Rao and David Shulman (1994). *When God is a Customer: Telugu Courtesan Songs by Ksetrayya and Others*. Berkeley and Los Angeles: University of California Press.

Rao, Velcheru Narayana and David Shulman (tr.) (1998). *A Poem at the Right Moment: Remembered Verses from Premodern*

South India. Berkeley, Los Angeles, London: University of California Press.

Spelman, Elizabeth V. (1982). 'Woman as Body: Ancient and Contemporary Views'. *Feminist Studies* 8 (1), pp. 109–31. https://doi.org/10.2307/3177582.

Shah, Shalini (2002). 'In the Business of Kāma: Prostitution in Classical Sanskrit Literature from the Seventh to the Thirteenth Centuries.' *The Medieval History Journal* 5 (2). https://doi.org/10.1177/0971945802005001.

———— (2009). 'Engendering the Material Body'. *Social Scientist* 47 (7/8), pp. 31–52. https://www.jstor.org/stable/26778565. Accessed 2 April 2023.

Shulman, David Dean (1980). *Tamil Temple Myths: Sacrifice and Divine Marriage in the South Indian Saiva Tradition.* New Jersey: Princeton University Press.

———— (1990). *Songs of the Harsh Devotee: The Tēvāram of Cuntaramūrttināyanār.* Philadelphia: University of Pennsylvania.

———— (1992). 'Poets and Patrons in Tamil Literature and Literary Legend'. In Barbara Stoler Millerm ed., *The Powers of Art. Patronage in Indian Culture.* Delhi: Oxford University Press, pp. 89–119.

Sivramkrishna, Sashi (2005). *The Curse of Talakad: (Re) situating and (Re)contextualizing a Legend in History.* Delhi: Rupa Publication Pvt. Ltd.

Śrītaraṉ, N. (2013) *Kāḷamēkap pulavar taṉip pāṭalkaḷ.* Ceṉṉai: Kaṅkai Puttaka Nilaiyam.

Subramaniyam, M.S. (2020). *Tirukkumaraṉaṭiyārkaḷ.* Ceṉṉai: Giri Trading Agency.

Tacarataṉ, Ā. (1994). *Tamiḻil vacaip pāṭalkaḷ (Āṇṭāṉ Kavirāyaṉ taṉip pāṭalkaḷ).* Ceṉṉai: Tamiḻ ōlaiccuvaṭikaḷ pātukāppu maiyam.

Tschacher, Torsten (2011). 'Method and Theory in the Study of Caṅkam (Sangam) Literature.' *Orientalistische Literaturzeitung* 106 (1). http://doi:10.1524/olzg.2011.0002.

Tamil Lexicon. Madras: University of Madras (1924–36).

Vaittiyanātan, Ec., ed. (1986). *Piṟkālap pulavarkaḷ.* Cennai: Makāmakōpāttiyāya tāṇṭar U. Vē. Cāminātaiyar nūl nilaiyam.

Venkataramaiah, K.M., ed. (1993 [1981]). *Civaṉ aruḷtiraṭṭu: tēvāram tiruvācakam tiruppukaḻ tiruvaruṭpā*. Durban: Natal Tamil Vedic Society, pp. 332–4,

Westkott, M. (1986). *The Feminist Legacy of Karen Horney*. New Haven, CT: Yale University Press.

Zvelebil, Kamil (1973). *The Smile of Murugan. On Tamil Literature of South India*. Leiden: Brill.

Zvelebil, Kamil (1974). *Tamil Literature*. Wiesbaden: Otto Harrassowitz.